PEACE IS A PROCESS

A Quaker effort to prevent the Crimean War, 1854

Deputation to CZAR NICHOLAS St Petersburg 1854
to try to CRIMEAN WAR
avert the

O mighty Prince may the miseries
+ devastation of war
be averted

Robert Charleton
Henry Pease
Joseph Sturge

Speak
truth
to power

A panel from the Quaker Tapestry
by Mary Mason and family

Swarthmore Lecture 1993

PEACE IS A PROCESS

Sydney D Bailey

Quaker Home Service
&
Woodbrooke College
for the
Swarthmore Lecture Committee

First published July 1993
by Quaker Home Service
and Woodbrooke College
for the Swarthmore Lecture Committee

ISBN 0 85245 249 7

Cover design by John Blamires

Preface

The Swarthmore Lectureship was established by the Woodbrooke Extension Committee at a meeting held December 9th, 1907: the minute of the Committee providing for an 'annual lecture on some subject relating to the message and work of the Society of Friends'. The name Swarthmore was chosen in memory of the home of Margaret Fox, which was always open to the earnest seeker after Truth, and from which loving words of sympathy and substantial material help were sent to fellow workers.

The lectureship has a twofold purpose: first, to interpret to the members of the Society of Friends their message and mission; and secondly, to bring before the public the spirit, the aims and fundamental principles of Friends. The lecturer alone is responsible for any opinions expressed.

The Swarthmore Lecture Committee, which administers the lectureship, is appointed by and reports to both Woodbrooke College Council and Quaker Home Service. The Committee arranges for the publication of a book and for the delivery of a lecture, the latter usually at the time of assembly of London Yearly Meeting of the Society of Friends. A lecture related to the present book was delivered in the Arts Centre Hall of the University of Warwick, on the evening of July 27th 1993.

Acknowledgments

My primary thanks are to my wife Brenda. She helped and supported me throughout the writing of this book and the preparation of the lecture. In many of the events referred to in the following pages we operated together, especially in Quaker work at the United Nations, participation in the conferences for diplomats, the founding of William Penn House, and numerous overseas trips. In spite of other demands on her time, she made many suggestions for adding to or deleting from the first and subsequent drafts. It is not only I, but you the reader, who is in her debt.

Much of the work for peace and justice in which Brenda and I have been engaged was supported by the Joseph Rowntree Charitable Trust. We take this opportunity of thanking trustees and staff for their support, financial and moral, over a period of more than thirty years.

The Swarthmore Lecture Committee appointed two 'minders', John Woods and Val Ferguson, to give me advice and encouragement. I am most grateful to them for their wise counsel at each stage.

Malcolm Thomas and his colleagues in the Library at Friends House were unfailingly helpful in tracking down obscure documents, recommending relevant books, suggesting illustrations, and in many other ways. Ted Milligan, a former librarian, was a constant source of inspiration and advice. Andrew Clark was of particular help regarding the section on Quaker war service.

In the early stages of drafting, Roger Wilson, in spite of failing health, made valuable suggestions and comments. Many others helped in various ways. I would mention in particular Herman Backman, Charlotte Blandford, Stephen Cary, Ellen Friis, the Reverend Keith Clements, Anna Sabine Halle, the Reverend Canon Anthony Harvey, Hope Hay Hewison, Barry Hollister, Lewis Hoskins, Alison Kelly, Sir John Lawrence, Mary Milligan, Sylvain Minault, Allan Parrent, the Rt Reverend Patrick Rodger, Elizabeth Salter, John Saunders, William Sessions, Keith Smiley, Donald Southall, Jack Sutters, Arthur White, and Duncan Wood.

To all of these friends and Friends I express deep gratitude.

January 1993   S.D.B.

CONTENTS

LIST OF ILLUSTRATIONS

Frontispiece: A Quaker effort to prevent the Crimean War, 1854. A panel from the Quaker Tapestry by Mary Mason and family. (Quaker Tapestry Scheme)

Page 81: Andrew Carnegie and Albert Smiley. (From the archives of the A. K. Smiley Public Library, Redlands, California)

Page 102: Meditation Room at the United Nations Headquarters, New York. (UN photo, ref no: 57,107)

Page 105: William Epstein and Otto Frey, joint heads of the United Nations Disarmament Section, and Sydney D. Bailey, outside the UN Security Council Chamber in 1956. (United Nations)

Page 108: Sydney D. Bailey presenting a set of his books on the United Nations to Secretary-General Waldheim. (United Nations, ref: Y Nagata)

Page 127: Agatha Harrison and Horace Alexander, members of the India Conciliation Group. (American Friends Service Committee)

Page 130: Russian Baptist pastors and their interpreters in Sweden in 1953; Aleksander Vasilievic Karev is on the left. (Sydney D. Bailey)

Page 148: Metropolitan Nikodim of the Russian Orthodox Church with a group of Friends at William Penn House, 1967. (Richard Haynes, by kind permission of his widow)

Introduction

My experience of Christian pacifism developed in three stages, and these are reflected in the three parts of this book.

I became a pacifist in 1930. An Anglican bishop had preached a sermon on Speech Day at my school, his text being taken from part of the reply of Jesus to the trick question about whether to pay taxes to the Roman emperor. The story is recounted in all three synoptic gospels, but the bishop took his text from the words in Mark's version: 'Render to Caesar the things that are Caesar's.' He told us that the essence of this reply of Jesus was that we owed a duty to the state, and that the most honourable way of discharging that duty, more noble even than taking Holy Orders, was to join the armed forces in order to defend and extend the British Empire.

At the age of fourteen, one has a limited understanding of how Christian ethics are to be practised in an ambiguous and complex secular world, but two things about the bishop's sermon troubled me. I understood why the bishop should think that the British Empire should be *defended*, but I could not see why he thought that it should be *extended*.

But what troubled me much more was that the bishop had nothing to say to us about the second part of the answer of Jesus: ' . . . and to God the things that are God's.' And it came to me in a flash of religious intuition that the way of Jesus is the way of peace.

This discovery was both inspiring and painful—inspiring because it threw light on other things that Jesus had said and done, painful because I thought I was the only person in the world who had concluded that true followers of Jesus should not take up arms. I refused thereafter to serve in the Officers' Training Corps, the only boy in the school to take this stand.

I knew the word *pacific*, but had not then heard the word *pacifist*. I eventually discovered the Fellowship of Reconciliation, and then the Society of Friends. The four books that particularly influenced me at this time were Beverley Nichols's *Cry Havoc*, A. A. Milne's *Peace with Honour*, G. H. C. Macgregor's *The New Testament Basis of Pacifism*, and Aldous Huxley's *Ends and Means*. I started attending Quaker meetings for worship in 1937, first at Carlton Hill in Leeds and then at Adel. By 1938, I was thinking of applying for membership, and probably would have done so but for the trend of the ministry at meeting on 2 October. That was the Sunday after the Munich Pact, which permitted Nazi Germany to take over the Czech Sudetenland. The Prime Minister,

Neville Chamberlain, had told us that this agreement ensured peace in our time. It was natural that we should heave a sigh of relief that war was averted, but I was troubled that so much of the ministry that Sunday should have been that the Munich Agreement was a victory for peace. How could a nation secure peace by letting down its friends? Had not true peace to be based on justice? You can see that I was in a mental muddle, for I had yet to learn that, even if one does what is right, innocent people may suffer. My attendance at Adel meeting became more sporadic, and I decided that I could never join the Society of Friends—a decision I was to revoke four years later. While I was in China with the Friends Ambulance Unit, I applied for membership on the overseas members list then kept by the Friends Service Council and was visited by an FAU colleague who was not then a Friend, Duncan Wood. My acceptance into membership seemed at the time like the end of a journey, but it was in fact only the beginning.

I realized in 1938 that war in Europe was inevitable. I decided that if military conscription were introduced, I would refuse to serve in the armed forces, even if that meant breaking the law. I had no conscientious objection to performing humanitarian service under civilian control, and I began to train as an air raid warden. The Nazis invaded Poland on my twenty-third birthday, and shortly after Chamberlain's speech to the effect that we would be at war with Germany at 11 a.m. on the Sunday morning, the air raid sirens sounded. I kissed my relatives good-bye before leaving for my post. We thought then that massive air raids would totally destroy cities, but it was not until the nuclear attack on Hiroshima six years later that such horrific destruction occurred.

During the nine-year period 1930 to 1939, I had thought that Christian pacifism simply meant saying 'no' to all war. I didn't know what we should do about Hitler, but I believed that we could not eliminate one evil by committing another evil. This was in some ways an inadequate view, but it was sincerely held.

The second phase in the evolution of my understanding of Christian pacifism, reflected in the second part of this book, was my recognition of the obligation to relieve the suffering of war victims. I applied to join the Friends Ambulance Unit (FAU) and decided that when I was conscripted, I would register as a conscientious objector and ask for exemption from military service on condition of continuing in the FAU.

I was puzzled about how the tribunals could judge the sincerity of a man's ethical beliefs (women had not yet been conscripted). I therefore went to the Leeds tribunal during my lunch breaks on a number of occasions so as to understand the procedure as clearly as possible. The effect of this was to increase my sympathy for the members of the tribunal, a sympathy that quickly evaporated when my own turn came! Some of the men applying for exemption were afraid of danger, some did not want to interrupt their careers or to leave wives and children, some said that army pay was too low, some objected to the principle of compulsion, and some had no objection to fighting in history's final war at Armageddon but refused to fight for the kingdoms of this world; and most of the applicants were timid, inarticulate, and confused.

The Leeds tribunal was thought in the pacifist community to be excessively harsh. Judge William Stewart's favourite question was about what the applicant would do if he came upon a German soldier raping his sister, and I confess that I never heard a plausible and convincing answer.

My written application for CO status was quite brief. I stated my belief that war was incompatible with the life, teaching, and death of Jesus of Nazareth; that as a follower of Jesus, I had a conscientious objection to serving in the armed forces; that I wished to perform humanitarian service under civilian control and had been accepted by the Friends Ambulance Unit. My application was heard by the tribunal on 11 March 1940.

Judge Stewart's first question concerned my religious affiliation. I had heard that Quakers had an easier time at CO tribunals than members of other Churches, but as I had decided that I would never apply to join the Society of Friends, I decided that I would not volunteer the fact that I occasionally attended Quaker meeting. So I replied that I was 'primarily a Christian'. At this comment, Judge Stewart visibly bristled.

There then followed a discussion of the difference between combatant and non-combatant service, after which Judge Stewart asked if I realized that only one man in a hundred was taking the CO position: 'the other ninety-nine have obeyed the law', to which I replied, 'So have I, sir, the law makes provision for conscientious objectors.' More bristling from the tribunal, this time not confined to Judge Stewart.

I was now asked whether it was a Christian act to go to the aid of the sick and wounded, to which I replied that it was certainly very Christian. 'If there was a wounded man in the street I would help him . . .' I was intending to say, 'whether he was a soldier or a civilian, whether he was British or German,' but Judge Stewart interrupted, 'I've heard all about that before.'

Judge Stewart concluded by paying tribute to my high ideals. If I were in a war zone as a member of the FAU and were captured, I would be shot because of my civilian status.* The tribunal was therefore removing my name from the Register of COs, and I would be called up for non-combatant military service. 'We are doing a very unusual thing in this case . . . but we are unanimous about it and are making a very strong recommendation for the RAMC' (Royal Army Medical Corps). I said I would appeal, to which Judge Stewart retorted 'I am deleting the recommendation. You can appeal if you like. Next case.'

My appeal was heard in London on 18 July 1940. Paul Cadbury was to have testified to my sincerity, but his journey from Birmingham was delayed by an air raid. The chairman of the appeal tribunal, Lord Fleming, began by asking me what I had done for humanity. I was initially a trifle nonplussed, and then I remembered that I had a certificate for having given twenty blood transfusions. The members of the tribunal treated me with great courtesy and consideration, and I was granted exemption from military service on condition that I did ambulance work under civilian control. I spent the next six years in the FAU, first in East London, then in Burma and China, then a year in the United States undergoing medical treatment, and then back in London.

The company for which I had worked before I was conscripted made up the salaries of men serving in the armed forces and kept jobs open for those who survived the war. In my case, the company was unwilling to make up the salary of a CO but said it would keep my job open. When I went to China, which was before Pearl Harbor, the company said it could no longer keep my job open as the war between Japan and China was 'not our war'. As things turned out, I was grateful for the decision: if my boring job had been held open for me, I would have felt an obligation to return to it after the war, and nothing was further from my thoughts when the time came to leave the FAU.

Pacifists found that there is no escape from ethical compromise in

*This was not correct: non-combatant medical personnel in war zones had protection under Article 9 of the Geneva Convention of 1929.

time of war. All of us in Britain paid indirect or direct taxes, knowing that part of the national revenue was used to finance the war effort. We all, civilians and combatants alike, ate food that had been brought to Britain in armed ships. I remember my shock at the beginning of the war when the police on traffic duty in Leeds had rifles slung over their shoulders. I travelled to the Far East in an armed merchant ship in a convoy with naval protection, including HMS *Repulse*, which was later sunk off Singapore.

Humanitarian work for war victims seemed to me an essential complement to the refusal to take up arms, but such service in war zones poses many moral problems, especially if one's own country is a belligerent. I examine some of these in the second part of this book.

★   ★   ★

After I left the FAU in 1946, I spent the next eight years working for Commander Stephen King-Hall, first as editor of his weekly *News-Letter* and then as secretary of the Hansard Society for Parliamentary Government. King-Hall had spent twenty years as a naval officer and had later been an independent Member of Parliament, being defeated by Harold Wilson at Ormskirk in 1945. During my time with him, King-Hall's ideas about defence were moving in a radical direction. He had come to the conclusion that modern weapons had made war obsolete, and he wanted people to break through the thought barrier (as he often put it) and take seriously the possibility of non-violent defence. He was what I came to call a pragmatic pacifist, though not a pacifist for moral reasons. 'The pacifist [he wrote] is not interested in countering violence, he is concerned with his conviction that violence as such is morally wrong.' King-Hall advocated 'Defence without Arms' as a practical policy for Britain. The object of war, he wrote, is not to kill or disable enemy combatants or to capture territory, but 'to change the enemy's mind.' He wanted to alter the basis of British defence strategy 'from one of violence to one of non-violence', involving careful planning and the training of the whole population in the techniques of non-violence. The ethic of the non-violent resister defeats the enemy by love and compassion, he wrote, and not by hatred.

Pacifists had his respect and admiration, 'and I am bound to say I think they have the teachings of Jesus on their side.' He believed that those who were pacifists for moral reasons were without influence on policy, but he did not see why pacifist ideas should be ignored by non-pacifists if they were useful for defence purposes.[1]

By 1954, I had been a pacifist for twenty-four years, and I began to ask myself whether it was enough to refuse to bear arms and to help the victims of war. Was it not also one's obligation to do all within one's capability to remove the causes of war and build a peaceful world? Brenda and I came to realize that, for some Friends, this was a full-time task. We therefore offered for the posts at Quaker House in New York, which is part of the set-up for Quaker work at the United Nations. Since then, I have worked mainly under Quaker auspices.

The task of the peace-maker is a daunting one, for pacifists are a minority in every country in the world—less than one per cent of the male population of Britain at the end of the second world war. Quaker peace-workers are accountable to a small but committed minority: governments, on the other hand, are responsible to those who voted them into power, those who voted for other parties, and those who did not vote at all. Friends can focus without compromise on a small range of issues: governments have to deal with almost everything, making concessions on some matters in order to gain advances on others.

The challenge for the Society of Friends is to find distinctive kinds of peace witness and action, accepting the fact that there are many important things that we will have to leave undone. We have to learn to work with others, including non-pacifist peace-lovers, as well as with those who (for want of a better word) we can only call militarists. Indeed, it was from my militarist friends from other Christian traditions that I discovered how seriously I had misunderstood the Just War ethic. I had assumed that a Just War was simply a label one attached to a war in which one's own side was engaged in order for it to seem justified. I learned from non-pacifist Christians that the Just War tradition had originated with Augustine of Hippo after the Emperor Constantine had embraced the Christian religion, and that it had been systematized by Thomas Aquinas in the Middle Ages. Aquinas, like Augustine, started from the assumption that war is opposed to charity and therefore is normally sinful, but he then posed the question 'whether it is *always* a sin to wage war' (my italics).[2] Aquinas then sets out a series of strict conditions that must be satisfied before going to war, as well as limitations on the conduct of military operations so as to minimize harm to the innocent. The Just War tradition, in other words, consists of restrictions and not permissions. It has not been tried and found wanting: it has been found difficult and left untried.

My own commitment to Christian pacifism is unshaken, but I have found it easier to engage in fruitful dialogue with strict Just War Christians than with pragmatic pacifists like Stephen King-Hall.

This has a bearing on the stance that Friends should adopt towards international treaties designed to protect war victims, such as the Geneva (Red Cross and Red Crescent) Conventions. Some Friends have taken the line that we have no business engaging in activities to make war more humane: our job is to abolish war. My own conviction is that our task is indeed to abolish war; but that in the meantime, it is a proper Quaker activity to seek to reduce the harm that will occur should war break out, by working to eliminate the more horrific weapons and to work also for humanitarian systems for the protection of war victims.

When I first became active in ecumenical affairs in 1952, I encountered some suspicion that pacifists might be disloyal, always finding fault with their own side and giving the other side the benefit of the doubt—the Nazis from 1933 to 1945, the Communists after the outbreak of the Cold War. There was no answer to this charge except to operate in accordance with a clear and consistent set of principles.

Peace-workers have to become well informed about issues of peace and war, but without recourse to networks of embassies, research departments, and intelligence services which foreign offices take for granted. At the same time, we must ensure that technical expertise does not smother Quakerly concern or separate us from those members of the Society who are called to other forms of witness and service.

We have to accept that in a world of radical and rapid change, our priorities and methods must change too. Who could have believed a decade ago that the Bolshevik Empire would disintegrate, that South Africa would begin to dismantle *apartheid*, that Middle Easterners would start negotiating about peace, that a draft treaty to prohibit chemical weapons would be signed, that a dialogue would begin between the two Korean states, that several sovereign states would invite UN observers to verify that their elections were free and fair, and that most Latin American states would agree that Latin America should be kept free of nuclear weapons? Political changes of this magnitude mean that Quaker agencies have to constantly re-appraise their allocations of money and personnel.

We must learn to deal creatively with conflict, both within the Society of Friends and between rival communities and nations. We need the patience to work persistently for goals that will almost certainly not be achieved in our lifetimes—general and complete disarmament, say, or universal respect for human rights. We have to discover ways of working for short-term advances without losing sight of our commitment to long-term objectives, to end the testing of nuclear weapons without abandoning the objective that *all* outward weapons will be abandoned in a world that uses only peaceful means for resolving conflicts and achieving justice.

Non-pacifists and pacifists alike are prone to hubris, non-pacifists in time of war, pacifists in time of peace. We Friends should not be ashamed to admit that we do not know all the answers, that we are no less perplexed than the rest of humankind when faced with gross evil, that some problems seem—in human terms—to be insoluble. Even when we know the direction in which to move, we Quakers can touch only the fringes of problems. But our commitment to peace and justice should be infectious, so that we inspire others to share in the process.

We invite each applicant for membership in the Society of Friends to become 'a humble learner in the school of Christ',[3] but we have much to learn from adherents of other Faiths and from those who reject all religion but still yearn for a peaceful and just world. We do not weaken our own spiritual and moral base by listening to others, for they may have insights that have eluded us. Indeed, listening is a crucial and creative element in all peace-making.

So this book seeks to illustrate three aspects of the Quaker peace testimony: the refusal to use outward weapons, the obligation to help the victims of war, and the call to become peace-makers.

1

FRIENDS SAY NO TO OUTWARD WEAPONS

I. FRIENDS SAY NO TO OUTWARD WEAPONS

What we now call the Quaker peace testimony has three components, and I would like to deal first with what the secular world may consider a negative stance: the refusal to bear arms, to undertake military training or service, to make or sell weapons of war.

THE BIRTH OF QUAKERISM
Quakerism arose in Britain in the middle of the seventeenth century, at a time of great questioning in all spheres of life—science, politics, religion. The House of Commons had rebelled against an autocratic king. In 1649, Charles I had been executed, the monarchy abolished as unnecessary and burdensome, and the House of Lords as useless and dangerous. Four years later, Oliver Cromwell was named Lord Protector.

It was in this situation of intellectual and political ferment that the Society of Friends was born. In the first decade, the 1650s, a body of belief and practice gradually began to emerge, but not always coherently and consistently. The peace testimony was initially little more than a belief that war was caused by greed, and that true followers of Jesus, having renounced greed, could not be the cause of war. When George Fox was asked to take up arms in defence of the Commonwealth in 1651, he replied in the well-known words: ' . . . I told them . . . I lived in the virtue of that life and power that took away the occasion of all wars'.[4]

THE EVOLUTION OF THE PEACE TESTIMONY
Political discontent began to develop after the death of Oliver Cromwell, and in 1660 the monarchy was restored and Charles II came to the throne. It was this that led to the first corporate statement of the Quaker testimony against war. There had been an uprising of the Fifth Monarchy Men in London, described by Samuel Pepys in his diary entries for 7 to 10 January 1661. Thomas Venner, the leader of the insurrection, was captured and, on 19 January, hanged, drawn, and quartered outside the Fifth Monarchy meeting house in Coleman Street. In the panic following this event, many Friends were arrested: it is believed that 4,257 Quaker men were in prison at this time, probably one-third of the total male membership of the Society.[5] In order to rebut the suspicion, totally unfounded, that Friends were implicated in the plot, George Fox and Richard Hubberthorne drafted a declaration of loyalty—or, rather, a denial of disloyalty—and this was presented to

Charles II on 21 January, two days after the execution of Venner.

By the standards of today, it is a long, rambling, and repetitive document, lavishly provided with quotations from scripture. Of the 2,000 words of the original document, fewer than 100 appear in London Yearly Meeting's current Book of Discipline. Friends, it says, 'utterly deny all outward wars and strife and fightings with outward weapons, for any end or under any pretence whatsoever.' The declaration goes on to stress that this is a consistent attitude, not to be practised or abandoned as political convenience dictates; but that the spirit of Christ will never move Friends to fight with outward weapons, neither for the kingdom of Christ nor for the kingdoms of this world.[6] The early Quaker assertion that wars arise from lusts (or 'the aggressiveness of your bodily desires', as the New English Bible has it) was simply to echo the epistle of James.[7] This seems to me to be a half-truth, for surely some wars have been fought from altruistic motives: wars to eliminate an evil that offends the human conscience such as slavery, wars to secure liberation from brutal and oppressive rule, wars under international auspices to resist aggression. I would be inclined to put the Christian pacifist position this way: that we will not use outward weapons even in just causes for two reasons, one reason primarily moral and one reason partially pragmatic. The moral reason is that human life is infinitely precious and should not be wantonly destroyed. The pragmatic reason is that it is folly to defeat evil with more evil, that wars, whatever the intention, almost always create as many problems as they solve. Our task must be to devise ways of resolving disputes without using lethal methods.

A second landmark in the evolution of the Quaker peace testimony came fifteen years after the declaration to Charles II, in the Latin edition of Robert Barclay's erudite *Apology*. Barclay starts firmly from the Sermon on the Mount. He admits that, before Christ, 'some things . . . were lawful to the Jews, considering their condition and dispensation.' But such things are forbidden to the disciples of Christ, who are to observe the most perfect charity and willingness to suffer. Barclay points out that this was the judgment of most Christian writers during the first three centuries of the Christian era. He then buttresses his conclusion with several quotations from the Bible. He states six objections to the Quaker position, and answers each. His conclusion is that it is not lawful for true Christians to defend themselves by arms, 'but they ought over all to trust to the Lord.'[8]

A third landmark in the evolution of our Quaker peace testimony did not come until the middle of the eighteenth century. At that time, quarterly meetings (now called general meetings) replied each year in writing to queries from Yearly Meeting. In 1742, there was included a query about military service: 'Do you bear a faithful and Christian testimony . . . against bearing arms?' The wording of the query was changed in 1860, perhaps because of difficulties over Quaker witness during the Crimean war, from 'against bearing arms' to 'against all war'. The testimony was no longer described as 'Christian' in the 1928 revision, but war was now described as 'inconsistent with the spirit and teaching of Christ'. In the 1967 revision, 'all preparation' for war was added as something against which Friends were called to witness.

A WAY FOR ALL OR A VOCATION FOR SOME?
One question faced by early Friends was whether the refusal to bear arms was a vocation for those who had chosen to pursue Christian perfection, comparable to the rule of celibacy for Roman Catholic priests and nuns, or whether it was a public policy to be practised by all rulers, or at least by all Christian rulers. During the 1650s, Quaker attitudes to the use of armed force were ambivalent. In 1659, Edward Burrough issued a letter to the army, urging soldiers to avenge innocent blood throughout the dominions controlled by Pope Alexander VII. Burrough advised officers to be loving, kind, and gentle, and ordinary soldiers to be sober, moderate, and faithful to the Lord.

> [I]f you honour him . . . he will honour you and set you atop of all your Enemies . . . If you dwell in the power of the Lord, you will be victorious over all your enemies, and the Lord will make you a dread and a fear to the nations.

But Burrough also stresses that there is 'a Kingdom which is not of this World, which cannot be obtained by an Outward Sword.' Better than fighting is to destroy the kingdom of the devil and the ground of wars.[9]

This ambiguous stance of Burrough was gradually to develop into what we would now call vocational pacifism. Isaac Penington, writing two years after Burrough and in the same year as the declaration to Charles II, was careful not to condemn those who used the sword in defence of justice, 'for this the present estate of things may and doth require . . . but yet there is a better state, which the Lord hath already brought some into, and which Nations are to expect and travel towards.' A good principle must have a beginning, he wrote, before it can grow and be perfected: it begins with an individual, spreads across the nation by degrees, 'and then from nation to nation, until the whole earth be leavened'.[10]

This was also the position taken by Robert Barclay. The magistrates of the Christian world, he wrote, were 'far from the perfection of the Christian religion' and had not 'come to the pure dispensation of the gospel.' While they were in that condition, it was impossible to say that war, 'undertaken upon a just occasion, is altogether unlawful to them', for 'they cannot be undefending themselves' (as Barclay put it) until they attain perfection.[11]

This view of Quaker pacifism as a vocation is expressed repeatedly in the laws of Pennsylvania until the middle of the eighteenth century: 'the people called Quakers who, though they do not, as the world is now circumstanced, condemn the use of arms in others, yet are principled against it themselves.'[12]

DOES GOD PROTECT THE RIGHTEOUS?

Many Friends seem to have believed that those who are faithful to the gospel will be protected by divine providence. Robert Barclay concluded his discussion of war by writing that those who are obedient to the precepts of the gospel 'ought over all to trust to the Lord.' Jonathan Dymond, a century and a half later, believed that, as it was God's plan that war should disappear from human society, divine providence would protect those who refused on grounds of conscience to defend themselves.

> We have his promise that he will protect those who abandon their seeming interests in the performance of his will; and we have the testimony of those who have confided in him, and he has protected them.

When Jack Catchpool was arrested while on a peace mission in Russia in 1918, he was confident that God would protect him.[13] Personally, I doubt that God intervenes in human affairs to protect those who do what is right.

I have come across a few Friends who think of non-violence as a kind of magic, a technique that inevitably evokes a non-violent response from the other person. When God told Joshua, 'I have given unto thine hand Jericho,' the children of Israel followed God's instructions: the priests blew the trumpets and the people gave a great shout, and 'the wall fell down flat.'[14]

But non-violence is not a kind of Old Testament miracle. I believe that God calls Friends to practise non-violence, but that means that we must be prepared to suffer and accept that others may suffer also. (The non-pacifist is in the same situation and must accept the fact that when violence is used, the innocent may suffer.) In the very short term, the crucifixion was a defeat, but in the long term a victory.

I believe that William Penn apprehended a crucial element in the Christian message with his phrase, 'Not Fighting, but Suffering'.[15] Jesus was vulnerable, exposed to physical and moral dangers, ran risks, accepted disappointment and suffering. He consorted with unpopular elements in society rather than with the Roman and Jewish élites. He disregarded ridicule. The crux of his message was love and forgiveness. Those who follow Jesus are not promised a safe or easy passage through life. We should not expect physical security. We go through life defenceless. What we *can* say is that God's goodness will triumph only when men and women act rightly, starting with me now.

WAR TAXES: THE STANCE OF BRITISH FRIENDS
An important issue of concern to Friends from the early days to the present has been whether to pay taxes to the secular authorities, knowing that part is spent on military matters. The first generation of Friends in Britain based their practice on the reply of Jesus to the question about the lawfulness of paying taxes to the Roman emperor. George Fox wrote: 'To the earthly we give the earthly: that is, to Caesar we give unto him his things, and to God we give unto Him His things.' If Friends did not pay taxes, the government might say, 'How can we defend you against foreign enemies . . . and keep down thieves and murderers?' The London Yearly Meeting epistle of 1693 declared:

> You very well know . . . our Christian Principles and Profession . . . both with respect to God and Caesar, That because we are subjects of Christ's Kingdom, which is not of this World, we cannot fight . . . Yet, being Subjects of Caesar's Kingdom, we pay our Taxes, Tribute, etc. according to the Example of Christ and his holy Apostles relating to Christ's Kingdom and Caesar's, wherein we are careful not to offend . . .

When Thomas Story spoke with the Tsar Peter the Great in London in 1697, he stressed that British Friends freely paid taxes to Caesar, 'for it is Caesar's part to rule, in justice and in truth, but ours to be subject, and mind our own business, and not to meddle with his.'[16]

WAR TAXES: THE PREDICAMENT OF AMERICAN FRIENDS

It was all very well for British Friends to say, 'Render unto Caesar the things that are Caesar's,' but in parts of North America, Friends *were* Caesar, for Quakers dominated the political life of Rhode Island and Pennsylvania for the best part of two generations. William Penn thought of Quakerism as a revival of the uncomplicated Christianity of the first three centuries. Early Christians led simple lives, preoccupied with the need to be faithful to the high standards of the gospel, and mainly concerned with family and church life. They waited for the imminent return of Jesus Christ to inaugurate God's perfect kingdom, taking no active part in the public affairs of the Roman Empire. Their attitude to the secular world of Caesar was ambivalent, for they believed it to be ordained of God and therefore to be obeyed: at the same time, the actual Caesars behaved wickedly, not least by persecuting the Church. What never entered their heads was that Caesar might one day become a Christian.

Then, to their astonishment, the Emperor Constantine embraced the Christian religion in 312 AD, and Christianity became in effect the state religion of the Roman Empire, shattering the Christian presuppositions of three centuries.

I wish we knew more about what Christian leaders said to Constantine. Did they point to the Sermon on the Mount and say that *that* was how a Christian ruler should govern? Or did they ask Constantine to protect church property and promote their friends to be bishops? From what is known of the subsequent history of the Roman Empire under Constantine, and of the teaching of Ambrose and Augustine between 380 and 430, it seems to me unlikely that Christian leaders pointed to the strenuous demands of the Sermon on the Mount.

To the early Friends, and especially to Penn, the Church had made a disastrous compromise in the fourth century, and true Christianity had been kept alive since then by fringe sects. Penn wished to revive what he called primitive Christianity, but with this crucial difference: he wanted Friends to be fully involved in the ambiguous world of national and international politics. 'True Godliness don't turn men out of the World, but enables them to live in it better, and excites their

The Friends Meeting House in Philadelphia and the Court House in which the Provincial Assembly met.

endeavours to mend it.'[17] He intended that Pennsylvania should be run in accordance with the high standards which he believed that Jesus demanded of his followers. Pennsylvania was to be what he termed a Holy Experiment,[18] but this was easier to declare in intention than to implement in practice. What were to be the implications of this in a province most of whose inhabitants refused on grounds of conscience to bear arms? Was military defence to be left to those citizens who had no scruples about fighting with outward weapons? And if so, was the expense to be met only by those citizens who had no conscientious objection to fighting or should the cost be shared equitably?

The question of taxation for military purposes in Pennsylvania had such crucial implications for Quaker witness that it is worth reviewing the saga in some detail. The issue first arose in 1689 when a request was received that Pennsylvania should make preparations for defence against an expected French attack. The initial reaction of the Quaker members of the Council was to belittle the gravity of the threat. Said John Simcock, 'I see no danger but from the bears and wolves.' When the issue could no longer be evaded, the Quakers decided to state their personal attitudes as a matter of conscience and to abstain from voting, but Simcock made it clear that they did not want to tie the hands of others; 'they may do every one what they please'.[19]

In 1693, Governor Benjamin Fletcher requested funds from Pennsylvania for the defence of New York, but he agreed that those who had scruples about supporting the war could give money which might be used for other purposes and 'not to dipt in blood'. The Quaker-dominated Assembly refused to vote funds until other matters had been attended to, but in the end a tax was approved, half to go to Governor Fletcher and half to the Crown. The latter was described as a 'free gift' and a testimony of affection for King William and Queen Mary.[20]

At home, Penn was under a cloud after William and Mary's accession to the throne because of his friendship with the discredited James II, and in 1693, Pennsylvania had been taken from him and joined to New York. Penn's struggle to have the province restored was successful in 1694. Penn was to pay an annual rent of 'two Beaver Skins, and the fifth part of the Gold and Silver Oar found in the limits of the said Tract of Ground'.

The Crown required Penn to provide a quota of 'Eighty Men with their Officers or the value of the charges of Maintaining the Same' for the defence and security of the Province. Penn agreed that he would 'carefully transmit to the Council and Assembly there all such orders as shall be given by their Majesties . . . and he doubts not but they will at all times dutifully comply with and yield obedience thereunto . . . for the supplying of such quota of men, or the defraying their part of such charges as their Majesties shall think necessary.' One wonders why Penn thought that his co-religionists in Pennsylvania would comply with the Crown's demands for military defence. Isaac Sharpless, the distinguished historian of Quaker politics in Pennsylvania, regarded Penn's commitment as disingenuous. 'It looks as if he intended to promise a course of action for the future, and then to unload this promise upon a body which would not redeem it.'[21]

When the Governor of Pennsylvania needed funds for defence, he now told the Friends that their contribution would be used to provide food and clothing for distressed Indians. Friends responded with a variety of prevarications: they wanted a new constitution first (1694), the assembly could not meet until the harvest was in (1695), they had contributed the previous years (1697), they were too poor to pay new taxes (1701).[22] When the issue of defence arose in 1709, the Quakers held an informal meeting to decide their attitude: ' . . . notwithstanding their profession and principles would not by any means allow them to bear arms; yet it was their duty to support the Govmt of their Sovereign the Queen . . . and therefore that they might and ought to present the Queen with a proper sum of money.' Governor Charles Gookin had suggested that an appropriate sum would be £4,000, but the Assembly thought that £500 would be enough. This led to a sharp response from Gookin: 'Words alone, I assure you, Gent., are not much valued by the ministry at Home, and £500 from Pennsylvania will add . . . but little weight.' The Quakers might have scruples about war, he said, but that should not prevent them from being generous in their gifts to the Queen. No conscience could be pleaded to prevent the grant of a sum 'in some measure worthy of Her Royal acceptance.' The response of the Assembly was to adjourn! In 1711, £2,000 was voted 'for the Queen's use.' Isaac Norris said, 'We did not see it to be inconsistent with our principles to give the Queen money, notwithstanding any use she might put it to; *that* not being our part, but hers.'[23] This now became the standard ploy—to appropriate funds as a gift for the Sovereign. In 1745 money was voted 'for the King's use' as a demonstration of 'loyalty and hearty affection for the Crown', the money to be spent on food 'and other grains'. Benjamin Franklin maintained that Gover-

nor George Thomas interpreted 'other grains' to mean gunpowder![24]
The final phase of Quaker control of Pennsylvania began in 1754. The Governor, Robert Hunter Morris, tried to introduce compulsory military service, with the option of making a grant for the King's use by those who objected on ground of conscience to bearing arms. The Assembly offered to set a tax, but on conditions that the Governor was unwilling to accept. New elections were held, and the Assembly proceeded to vote funds for the relief of friendly Indians and distressed frontiersmen. The money was, in fact, mainly spent on building a chain of forts.[25]

WOOLMAN AND SOME OTHER TAX OBJECTORS

By now, a number of Friends had become uneasy about the practice of appropriating money for the King's use, knowing that it would be used for military purposes. John Woolman admitted that it was not a pleasant thing for young Friends to question the judgment or honesty of their respected elders 'but it is the duty of everyone to be firm in that which they certainly know is right for them.' Woolman was particularly distressed that when Friends withheld war taxes on grounds of conscience, their goods were distrained by other Friends. Twenty Friends, including Woolman, addressed a letter to the Pennsylvania Assembly on the subject of war taxes. The signatories had no objection to paying taxes to cultivate the friendship of Indians or for other benevolent purposes, but to put money into the hands of committees which applied it to purposes inconsistent with the peaceable testimony of Friends was destructive of religious liberty. The signatories considered that many of them would be 'under the necessity of suffering, rather than consenting thereto.' The matter came up at Philadelphia Yearly Meeting and a committee was appointed, but Friends were deeply divided on the issue. Finally, the committee reported that it had had 'several weighty and deliberate conferences' but had found 'diversity of sentiments'. It had unanimously concluded 'that it is not proper to enter into a public discussion of the matter.' Friends were urged to 'endeavour earnestly to have their minds covered with fervent charity towards one another.'[26]

FRIENDS RENOUNCE CONTROL OF PENNSYLVANIAN POLITICS

During this final period of Quaker control, British Friends were unhappy about the acerbic style of Pennsylvanian Quakers on the tax issue. This is illustrated in some of the letters from Dr John Fothergill to Israel Pemberton, Jr in Philadelphia.

> Your cause is undoubtedly good, but I am afraid you discover a little more warmth than is quite consistent with the moderation we profess . . . (8 April 1742)
> But I would just take leave to observe, and that with the utmost deference, that a good cause may suffer by too passionate a vindication . . . (18 August 1755)
> I dislike servile obsequiousness but a respectful condescension to those to whom in the course of providence we are connected in some degree of subordination is by no means unbecoming (4 October 1755).[27]

When John Fothergill's younger brother Samuel was visiting America, he also was struck by the lack of civility and respect with which the Quakers addressed the Governor. He urged that Friends should withdraw from politics 'and live in peace and quietness, minding their own business as Friends do every where else', for he could not see how Friends could be faithful to the testimony against war 'without being loudly cried against'. He feared that Friends in Pennsylvania were motivated by 'The love of power, the ambition of superiority, the desire of exemption from suffering.'[28]

Lord Granville, Lord President of the Council in Britain, told John Fothergill that if the Quakers did not provide for the defence of Pennsylvania, the Assembly would be dissolved, and a Bill sponsored by the Secretary of War, Lord Barrington, would prevent Quakers from standing for re-election by the requirement that members of the Pennsylvania assembly would in future have to take an oath of allegiance. John Fothergill described the view of the British Government in a letter to Israel Pemberton, Jr.

> You accept of a public trust which at the same time you acknowledge you cannot discharge. You owe the people protection and yet withhold them from protecting themselves.

British Friends thought that Friends in Pennsylvania should decide not to stand for re-election rather than wait to be totally excluded for ever.[29] The matter was considered by both London Yearly Meeting and Meeting for Sufferings in 1756, and it was decided to send two emissaries to Pennsylvania (John Hunt and Christopher Wilson) as bearers of a letter from Friends in Britain. The tone of the letter is rather like that of parents instructing tiresome children. The letter reported the belief in Britain, among both the lower and less discerning parts of the population and in the higher reaches of the Government, that the calamities befalling Pennsylvania proceeded from the principles and behaviour of the Quakers and their consequent failure to provide for the security of the Province, leading to widespread odium and resentment. A Bill had actually been drafted to exclude from any legislative assembly in America those who refused to take the oath of allegiance. The efforts of British Friends would undoubtedly have been ineffectual had not a person who held the Society of Friends in high regard (identified by John Fothergill as Lord Granville) been able to suspend the proceedings, which Friends in London esteemed a favourable interposition of Providence.

> This Short Suspension has not been obtained without considerable difficulty, and our Engaging to use our utmost endeavours with you to decline being chosen into Assembly during the present situation. We cannot but earnestly intreat your effective Compliance with the Expectations by us given.[30]

Some Friends in Pennsylvania, but not all, either resigned their seats or refused to stand for re-election, and Friends were now no longer in a majority. In 1758, Philadelphia Yearly Meeting advised Friends not to accept any office in civil society or government in which they might have to encourage or compel others to perform acts which they themselves might conscientiously scruple to perform.[31] Since 1756, no government anywhere in the world has been controlled by members of the Society of Friends.

What is an *ad hoc* decision the first time it is taken easily becomes a precedent. When money was requested for military purposes, the first reaction of Friends in Pennsylvania was to deny that the situation was dangerous. When this argument had exhausted its utility, Friends claimed that the measures contemplated were provocative. If a request for funds were persisted in, they said that their grievances should be considered first, or that it was inconvenient for the Assembly to meet, or simply that they could not afford the money. When prevarication would no longer suffice, funds were usually voted, at first on the understanding that they would not be used for military purposes, but after 1709 simply as a present for the Sovereign.

The fact was that Pennsylvania could not be isolated from the external situation. The colony posed no threat to others, but the Quakers of that day learned, as each generation has learned since, that the task is not to create a peaceable kingdom as a sanctuary into which to escape from the wars and rumours of wars which afflict the rest of mankind. Refusal to bear arms is not enough: we must also build the institutions of peace—to use the title of Duncan Wood's 1962 Swarthmore Lecture.

Were British Friends right to urge the Quakers of Pennsylvania to withdraw from public affairs? Carl Heath, a passionate advocate of Quaker involvement in public life, 'infinitely regretted' the withdrawal of Pennsylvanian Quakers. In his Swarthmore Lecture of 1922, he described it as 'The descent into littleness': '. . . a problem is not solved by ceasing to try to solve it.' Heath does not indicate how Friends should have handled the dilemma they faced in 1756: he simply could not believe that withdrawal was an adequate response.[32] Konrad Braun, in the Swarthmore Lecture in 1950, suggested what the alternatives were. 'It would have been possible for them . . . to remain in office until either the Crown had deprived them of their rights or the constituency had withdrawn its support . . . '[33]

I, too, advocate participation and involvement in the affairs of the world, but I admit that this is to state a problem, not solve it.

WAR TAX REFUSAL

The most obvious way of saying 'no' to all war is not to use outward weapons. Another way is to refuse to pay taxes used *exclusively* for military purposes. There have been times in the past when that has been possible, and my impression is that Friends have almost always refused to pay such taxes since the *débâcle* in Pennsylvania. Nowadays, however, governments levy taxes for general purposes and then decide how the revenue shall be allocated to different functions.

Job Scott of Rhode Island noted in his journal in 1779 that Friends were unanimous against paying taxes used wholly for war; 'and many solid Friends manifested a lively testimony' against the payment of taxes used partly for civilian and partly for military purposes.[34]

During the American Civil War, an eccentric and somewhat quarrelsome member of Short Creek Monthly Meeting in Ohio, Joshua Maule, withheld part of his tax for five years. Maule had previously decided that the reading of newspapers was 'unprofitable and danger-

ous', tending to leave the mind in an unsettled state. He was at the time
the local postmaster, but he asked himself, 'How canst thou hand out
to others that which thou dost not think fit for thyself to read?' He
therefore gave up his job as postmaster. Some years later, he removed
from his library all books which he found objectionable, including
Macaulay's 'pernicious' *History of England*.[35]

When he came to pay his tax in 1861, he deducted 8½%, being the
part earmarked for war purposes. Others should do as they would, he
wrote, but the only safe way for him was to refuse to pay for war, and
take the consequences. A few weeks later, a neighbour asked for the
loan of a small sum of money, to which Maule readily agreed. The
neighbour then said he needed the money to pay Maule's 8½%. Maule
insisted on the return of the loan, which perplexed the neighbour.
Shortly after this, Maule's goods were distrained, and so 'what
appeared at first like a mountain of difficulty has passed comfortably
away, and renewed cause remains to trust in Him who careth for all
who fear and obey him.' The same procedure was followed in the four
succeeding years.[36]

The issue of earmarking or withholding that part of tax used for
military purposes arose for British Friends in 1982, when some members of the staff at Friends House objected on grounds of conscience
that a proportion of the national revenue, estimated at about 12%, was
spent on military preparations. There was no way of earmarking or
withholding a proportion of government revenue derived from such
sources as Value Added Tax or Customs and Excise Duties, but Meeting for Sufferings might have been able to earmark or withhold part of
the Pay As You Earn tax (PAYE) deducted from the salaries of staff at
Friends House, on the ground that to contribute to military defence
was contrary to the conscientious convictions of some staff members.
Meeting for Sufferings began withholding and earmarking 12% of the
PAYE of those staff who requested that this be done, and in 1985 the
Inland Revenue instituted legal proceedings to recover the amount
withheld. The case was heard in the County Court, which upheld the
Inland Revenue's claim. Friends then went to the Appeal Court, but
the Appeal was dismissed, as was an application to the Appeal Committee of the House of Lords.

The question then arose as to whether London Yearly Meeting could
take the matter to one of the international bodies concerned with the
protection of human rights. In the case of the UN Covenant on Civil

and Political Rights, the United Kingdom had not then (and still has not) accepted the procedure for petitions from individuals, but it was possible to appeal to the European Commission on Human Rights. In order to do this, applicants have to overcome two procedural obstacles. First, applicants must first have exhausted all domestic remedies: this Friends had done. Secondly, the Commission 'shall not deal with any petition [which] is substantially the same as a matter which has already been examined by the Commission.' The difficulty here was that the Commission had in 1983 rejected two applications almost identical to the one Friends were submitting.

In 1986, the clerk and a former assistant clerk of Meeting for Sufferings, Beryl Hibbs and Maisie Birmingham, submitted a formal application to the European Human Rights Commission, claiming that the denial of the option of earmarking taxes for specific purposes was a violation of the right to manifest religion or belief in practice and observance, as guaranteed by Article 9 of the Convention. In the course of the application, the two Friends referred to one of the 1983 cases which the Commission had rejected as inadmissible, but they 'respectfully' submitted that the Commission's decision in 1983 had been 'wrong'. Not surprisingly, the Commission took the same line as it had done three years previously. Having set out the facts and the law, the Commission found that there had been no interference in the rights guaranteed by the Convention. The complaint was 'manifestly ill-founded' and the petition was declared to be inadmissible.[37]

The question for London Yearly Meeting was what further action would be appropriate, and unity was not easily achieved. A few Friends wanted Meeting for Sufferings to withhold the 12% whatever the consequences. Others, probably a majority, believed that Friends should first try to get the law changed before resorting to such drastic action. Finally, in 1991, Meeting for Sufferings decided to pursue the matter within the law by sending a letter of protest each time income tax collected from the staff was transmitted to the Inland Revenue.

The 1991 decision was probably the only course open to Meeting for Sufferings in a situation in which Friends were divided. I and other Friends, believing that a denial of human rights is a frequent cause of armed conflict, had devoted much energy to the development of an effective international system for the protection of human rights. Friends resorted to that system by petitioning the European Commission on Human Rights, and the Commission had found the petition to be inadmissible. There was no higher court to which Friends could appeal other than the court of personal conscience. To have challenged the decision of the European Commission on Human Rights would, in my view, have had the effect of undermining the international structure for protecting human rights. Friends have never hesitated to break laws they consider immoral, but it is surely wise to try and get the law changed first.

The practical difficulty for the authorities about conscientious tax refusal or the earmarking of taxes for particular purposes is that to respect one sort of conscientious scruple almost certainly opens the door to a host of other conscientious scruples: Jehovah's Witnesses who object to the blood transfusion service, environmentalists who object to new motorways, religious fanatics who object to public money being used for schools run by another group of religious fanatics, and so on.

CIVILIAN ALTERNATIVES TO COMPULSORY MILITARY SERVICE

Friends have from time to time asked themselves whether it is appropriate to undertake civilian alternatives to military service. There was general agreement that it was wrong to employ substitutes or pay commutation fees in lieu of military service, and most British Friends have been unwilling to perform non-combatant duties in the armed forces. But since war became total, involving whole populations and not simply professional soldiers, and since governments have been able to organize conscription on a systematic basis, Friends corporately have tended to say two not wholly compatible things. First, that governments have no right to *compel* young men (and during the second world war in Britain, young women too) to perform military service; but that if compulsory military service should nevertheless be introduced, legal provision should be made to exempt from military service those with genuine conscientious scruples.

Compulsion for military service in Britain was, until the twentieth century, haphazard. During the first world war, however, conscription of men was introduced in 1916 on an organized basis. Just over 16,000 men claimed exemption on grounds of conscience, of whom some 21% served in the Royal Army Medical Corps or undertook other non-combatant duties in the armed forces, just under 10% served in the Friends Ambulance Unit or the Friends War Victims Relief Committee, and around 30% did civilian work 'useful for the prosecution of the war'. Over 6,000 men were arrested for defying the conscription regulations. Two different authorities estimate that about one in three of conscripted Quaker men served in the armed forces during the first world war.*[39]

Compulsory military service for men was introduced a few months before the outbreak of the second world war and continued for some years thereafter. Roger Wilson stressed in his Swarthmore Lecture in 1949 that the British Government and people were 'generous' to conscientious objectors during the second world war.[40] The tribunals for assessing the genuineness of conscience were, on the whole, much fairer than during the first war. My own experience during the second world war was that, the nearer one got to danger, the more tolerant people were of one's pacifist stance—more tolerant in London during the blitz than in the countryside or unbombed towns, more tolerant among the troops in war zones than among the bombed civilians in Britain.

My experience of ordinary British privates during the second war was that they were singularly free of hatred, either for those of us on our side who were 'conchies' or of the ordinary soldiers on the other side. Owen Stephens, an AFSC worker in France during the first world war, had a similar experience.

> It is unvaryingly true that as people come closer to the actual fighting, both in place and time, they lose their ill-feeling and hate and come more strongly to realize that the other fellow and themselves are exactly the same kind of persons . . . It is conceivably true that the more distant the connection of people with the actual fighting the more bitterness, prejudice, and hate they bear for the other side.[41]

Roger Wilson, writing of the second world war, had this to say.

> Speaking personally as a Christian pacifist, I had a far deeper sense of spiritual unity with those of my friends in the fighting services, who, detesting war as deeply as I did, yet felt that there was no other way in which they could share the agony of the world, than I had with those pacifists who talked as if the suffering of the world could

---

*Although precise figures are not available, it seems likely that about 70% of US Quakers who were drafted during the first world war served in combatant or non-combatant units in the armed forces.[38]

be turned off like a water tap if only politicians would talk sensibly together.[42]

At the beginning of the second world war, 20 in every thousand male conscripts claimed exemption from military service on grounds of conscience, but within a few months the proportion had fallen to 5 per thousand, and thereafter declined to 2 per thousand at the end of the war. The entry of the Soviet Union into the war, which had such a profound effect on Marxist and other left-wing attitudes, had a negligible effect on the proportion of men claiming to be COs. During the course of the war, just over 61,000 and 1,000 women claimed CO status.[43]

The issue of compulsion also arose in connection with fire-watching, which was introduced for men in 1941 and for women in 1942. Kathleen Lonsdale, a distinguished Quaker scientist, was perfectly willing to undertake fire-watching voluntarily and could have claimed exemption when it became compulsory. She refused on grounds of conscience to register for compulsory fire-watching, however, was fined, refused to pay the fine, and spent a month in Holloway gaol in 1943. She was then prosecuted again, and again fined £2 (about £50 in today's currency), again refused to pay the fine, and an anonymous person paid it for her. At that point, the authorities seem to have allowed the matter to drop.[44]

SOME BORDER-LINE CASES

There have been other issues that have troubled Friends in addition to taxation and alternative service. Were Quakers allowed to carry weapons, not to use, but to frighten? Amelia Mott Gummere recounts the case of four young members of Burlington Meeting in New Jersey early in the eighteenth century who went armed in search of escaped prisoners: 'it seemed best for those that had guns to take them, not with a design to hurt, much less to kill . . . but we thought that if we could meet these runaways, the sight of the guns might fear them.'[45]

For shipowners who were converted to Quakerism, there was the question whether to leave guns on their ships. Some Friends removed the guns willingly, some only reluctantly. A few kept the guns but took no ammunition to sea, and a few carried replica guns made of wood![46]

The testimony against bearing arms did not technically cover the manufacture or sale of weapons, for these could be used for hunting purposes. There was, however, considerable unease at the end of the eighteenth century when it was realized that the Galton family firm in Birmingham was supplying guns to the British Government. Friends wrestled with the Galtons, father and son, and in 1795 Samuel Galton senior severed his connexion with the firm. His son Samuel was more recalcitrant, however, maintaining that weapons are not the cause of war. In 1796, he was formally disowned, though he continued to worship with Friends. The Yearly Meeting epistle in 1798 called on Friends to show 'a peaceful and innocent demeanour amongst men; and especially let all be careful not to seek or accept profit by any concern in the preparations so extensively making for war.' Samuel Galton Jr. gave up the manufacture of weapons soon after this, and he was buried in the grounds of Bull Street Meeting House in Birmingham in 1832.[47]

Another issue for Friends was whether it was right to provide food and clothing for the armed forces. During the 1745 uprising in favour of the Young Pretender, Friends in Darlington are said to have provided the Army with 10,000 woollen waistcoats. During the Crimean War, C. and J. Clark of Somerset sold sheepskin coats to the Government for the use of the troops, but the profit of some £300 (about £11,000 in today's money) was donated for a new school in Street.[48]

DID GOD SANCTION OLD TESTAMENT WARS?
Barclay had maintained that some things that were forbidden to followers of Jesus were lawful to the Jews in Old Testament times 'considering their conditions and dispensation.'[49] A few Friends of advanced views at the beginning of the nineteenth century could not believe that God had *ever* sanctioned war. Abraham Shackleton, an Irish Friend from Ballitore in County Kildare, held that it was highly derogatory to the character of the unchangeable character of God to conceive that he would act in opposition to those moral laws that he had ordained to be of perpetual and universal obligation.

> Consequently, that neither wars, nor any acts of cruelty, treachery, or fraud . . . were ever either approved of, or authorized by the God of purity, holiness, peace and love.

The alleged commands of God in the Old Testament for perfidious or cruel acts were either wilful and impious pretences on the part of the perpetrators or recorders of the events, or subsequent interpolations:

School in Street built in 1859 with a contribution of £300 from C. and J. Clark.

'a right apprehension of, and due regard for, the divine attributes, would forbid our assent to such passages [of Scripture].' Shackleton's views shocked the Quaker Establishment, and he was disowned in 1801.[50] Hannah Barnard, a Quaker Minister from Hudson, New York, was travelling in the ministry in Europe and came in touch with Shackleton and others of like opinions. She also held firmly to the view 'that in no age of the world, the great and merciful Creator ever commissioned any nation or person to destroy another.' Like Shackleton, she could not accept those parts of the Old Testament in which God was said to have commanded the Jewish people to make war. In 1802, Hannah Bernard was also disowned.[51]

What did mainstream Friends mean in 1801–2 when they said that the Bible was 'true', thus implying that God approved or even commanded Old Testament wars? London Yearly Meeting's current *Book of Discipline* contains six extracts on the Scriptures. Four are from the first generation of Friends—Fox, Barclay, Hubberthorne, and Penington. Fox and Hubberthorne took a simple view. The Scriptures 'were given forth by the Holy Spirit of God, through the holy men of God' (Fox). Hubberthorne believed that the Scriptures were 'a declaration of truth.' Barclay, with greater subtlety, wrote that the Scriptures contain a faithful historical account of the actions of God's people, but that they are not to be esteemed the principal ground of all truth and knowledge; they are a secondary source, 'subordinate to the Spirit.' Penington urged us 'to make a right use of the Scriptures . . . esteeming them in their right place.'[52] I would certainly hope that those present members of London Yearly Meeting who share the views of Abraham Shackleton and Hannah Barnard about Old Testament wars will not find themselves disowned!

HOW CAN A TESTIMONY BECOME A POLICY?

In view of the many problems arising from our stand against outward weapons, I find it helpful to think of the Quaker peace testimony as a witness, a vocation, but not as a simple solution to a difficult problem. Our convictions are sincerely held, but replete with ambiguities, inconsistencies, and grey areas. We call for the negotiation of *partial* disarmament when most of us really favour *total* disarmament. We oppose weapons that are especially inhumane without always making clear our rejection of *all* weapons of war. I recall when Friends criticized the transfer of British troops from Cyprus to Malta, and then, a few years later, were equally critical when the troops were moved back from Malta to Cyprus: what we *really* meant, but failed to say, was that we rejected the whole notion of military defence, not the movement of troops from one Mediterranean island to another. The challenge is to work for partial but imperfect steps, while clearly maintaining our commitment to the perfectionist goals of the Sermon on the Mount.

Max Weber, the German sociologist, distinguished between an ethic of responsibility and an ethic of ultimate ends. An ethic of responsibility requires involvement in the dilemmas and ambiguities of the secular world, making choices by estimating the likely consequences of each act. 'No ethic in the world can dodge the fact that in numerous instances the attainment of "good" ends is bound to the fact that one must be willing to pay the price of using morally dubious means or at least dangerous ones.' He contrasted this with an ethic of ultimate ends which is concerned only in ensuring that the flame of pure intention is not quenched. He cited the Quakers in Pennsylvania and other radical pacifist sects as those who tried for a time to maintain an ethic of ultimate ends in the world of politics, though the experiment 'took a tragic course' when it came to be realized that 'the tasks of politics can only be solved by violence.' Weber's ethical dichotomy was very influential among mainstream church leaders in the early decades of the World Council of Churches.[53]

Weber's distinction between an ethic of motives and an ethic of consequences is, nevertheless, a useful one. Mike Yarrow, the author of a standard book on Quaker conciliation, insists that for Friends the emphasis of peace-making is on 'the intention behind the act rather than a calculation of consequences.'[54] We have to admit, of course, that individuals some of the time and governments most of the time are guided by Weber's ethic of responsibility. The calculation of consequences is inevitably a crude method of decision-making, for we usually do not have sufficient information to know what will happen in a variety of eventualities.

Weber argued that those who pursue an ethic of ultimate ends should not hope to do so along the avenue of politics. 'The genius or demon of politics lives in an inner tension with the god of love . . . ' But it seems to me that a chief task of Christian ethics is to set limits on the means that may be used to achieve righteous ends. Paul of Tarsus denied that the followers of Jesus were in favour of doing evil that good may come.

We need to distinguish between strategic and tactical decision-making. Our strategy arises from religious concern, what Weber called the pure flame of intention. At this level, we should not be deterred by fear of failure. But at the tactical level, it is sensible to assess likely consequences: it is stupid to go on a mediation mission if the leaders we wish to see will be away at a conference, or on holiday, or preoccupied with other pressing matters.

And if motive and not consequences is to guide our strategy, let us do our level best to live up to the strenuous commands of the Sermon on the Mount and the other teachings and example of Jesus. The flame of pure intention points towards a goal we shall never reach, and there may be several paths to that perfect goal.

Our critics would say that there is an anarchic streak in Quakerism, that we enjoy the benefits of free political institutions and yet ask to be exempt from the military service that is expected from our fellow citizens who, as Roger Wilson pointed out in his Pendle Hill lectures during the second world war, were '. . . fighting and dying, amongst other reasons, for our right to be pacifists . . .'[55]

Some of our critics would dismiss us as essentially irresponsible, unwilling to accept the obligations of Christian citizenship. The more understanding of our critics would perhaps admit that our witness points to a destination that peoples and nations should expect and travel towards, but that we have not yet got very far in devising policies that could be put before public opinion and implemented by the Caesars of the contemporary world. If we fail to express our principles in terms that make sense to decision-makers, we will remain on the fringes of political life.

T.S. Eliot wrote that human kind cannot bear very much reality.[56] The reality which the non-pacifist finds it hard to bear is that the use of armed force to defeat injustice, even when resorted to unselfishly and sacrificially, may engender new injustice: war may seem to one generation a terrible necessity, but it may create conditions that compel future generations to pay the price of more wars. The reality which the Christian pacifist finds it hard to bear is that love does not always 'work', that those who are immature, or mentally disturbed, or have themselves suffered grievous wrong, may be impervious to love: yet to express love in action, even when circumstances were unpropitious, was the way of Jesus, and the way to which he calls his followers.

In the seventeenth century, Friends were regarded as dangerous rebels—hence the Declaration to Charles II. Britain was aflame with religious and political dissent—Ranters, Muggletonians, Levellers, Diggers, Fifth Monarchy Men. Why have Friends survived as an organized body? Why have we changed from dangerous rebels to respectable rebels?

Perhaps part of the explanation is a matter of numbers, for we are no longer numerous enough to pose much of a threat to the rest of society. During the first generation of Quakerism, the number of Friends grew from zero to around 50,000, out of a total population of some 5 million. If the proportion of Friends in the population had remained constant during the past three centuries, there would today be half a million members of London Yearly Meeting. But the number of Friends has in fact dwindled to one-third of what it was in 1693, while the population of Britain has increased tenfold.

There are reasons for the transition from dangerous rebels to respectable rebels which are beyond the scope of this Swarthmore Lecture. Two, however, have a bearing on my main theme. We are no longer content simply to say 'no' to outward weapons, for we also play a small part in relieving the suffering of the victims of war and in seeking to build a world of justice and peace.

2

QUAKER WAR RELIEF

II. QUAKER WAR RELIEF

INDIVIDUAL INITIATIVES

Friends have coupled their refusal to fight with work to bind up the wounds of the victims of war, though for the first two centuries, such work was not institutionalized. Beginning in 1755, Anthony Benezet organized a relief scheme in Philadelphia for some 450 war refugees from Nova Scotia.[57] Twenty years later, during the War of American Independence (as I was taught to call it), Friends in America raised money for war relief.[58] During the Napoleonic Wars, several British Friends were active in their personal capacities in raising funds for relief on the continent, and other Friends gave pastoral care to Scandinavian POWs in the Medway area.[59] In 1822–3, William Allen and other Friends were active in helping Greek refugees from Khios who had rebelled against Turkish rule.[60] After the Crimean War, Joseph Sturge and Thomas Harvey undertook an exploratory journey to Finland, then part of Russia, to ascertain the relief needs of distressed civilians. They were able to raise substantial funds for famine relief and the 'reclamation and drainage of waste land and morasses, as one means of guarding against future chances of famine.'[61]

It would be tedious to describe all the war relief efforts of British and Irish* Friends, but I believe that lessons can be learned from Quaker war relief in four wars: a war in which the United Kingdom was not a participant (the Franco-Prussian war of 1870–1) and three wars in which the UK was a belligerent (the Anglo-Boer war of 1899–1902, and the two world wars, 1914–18 and 1939–45).

FRANCO-PRUSSIAN WAR

The first institutionalized programme of war relief by British and Irish Quakers came during the Franco-Prussian war of 1870–71, with the creation of the Friends War Victims Relief Fund. The aid was strictly limited to non-combatants, as many Friends had conscientious scruples about help being given to combatants who might then rejoin the fighting. It is believed that about £162,000 was raised for war relief (about £6 million in today's currency). Three-quarters of this was spent on seed-corn and other agricultural supplies, the balance on relief to

* A Yearly Meeting was established in Ireland in 1669, and Irish Friends have participated in most of the war relief referred to in the following pages. Dublin/Ireland Yearly Meeting joined with London Yearly Meeting in sponsoring the Council for International Service, the Friends Service Council, and Quaker Peace and Service. In 1992, it was decided that Quaker Peace and Service should become a department of London Yearly Meeting only, though in close association with Irish Friends.

the poor and gifts of money to local communities. The work was
mainly centred around Metz, in the Moselle *département* of north-east
France, though a small sum of money was distributed in the Saar
region of Germany. The workers, 33 men and 8 women, were known as
commissioners, 11 of them non-Friends. All except 10 paid their own
expenses, and most of them, like John Bellows, were 'business men
who could not spare more than a month away from their own affairs.'
One stayed only a week and several a fortnight, although eight did two
tours of duty. James Long (not a Friend) stayed for four years, repre-
senting Friends in France and engaging in a variety of humanitarian
activities. From 19 October 1870 to 8 May 1871, the home committee
met virtually every weekday for between two and five hours. Three of
the workers (Richard Allen, James Long, and Robert Spence Watson)
and three French colleagues were offered the French Legion of
Honour: Robert Spence Watson refused the award, so a special medal
was struck for him.[62]

It was during this episode of war relief that the Quaker star was
devised as a logo, initially with an inscription in English, French, and
German: this enabled relief supplies to enter France free of import duty
and to move on French railways at half price. Each worker carried a
document setting out the aims of the relief:

> The bearer of this document is sent out by the Religious Society
> known in England as the Society of Friends, commonly called
> Quakers, solely to give relief to the non-combatant sufferers through
> the present war.
> We, the members of the above-named Society of Friends, believe
> all war to be contrary to the Will and Spirit of our Heavenly Father,
> as shown in the New Testament; but, moved by Christian love, we
> desire to alleviate, as far as may be in our power, the misery of non-
> combatants, irrespective of nationality, remembering that all are
> children of One Father, and that One Saviour died for all.
> We therefore entreat all to whom the bearer may come to aid him
> in the fulfilment of his mission.

Ormerod Greenwood described the Quaker work during this period
as 'chaotic, uncoordinated, wasteful, sometimes sentimental.' There
were a number of reasons for the chaos, lack of coordination, and
waste. Organization in Britain was minimal, so the workers had to
make their own arrangements for travel, acquiring foreign currency,

Quakers' Relief Fund for Distressed Peasantry.

Pour le Sécours des Paysans dirigé par les Quakers.

Fond zur Hülfe der Landleute unter Verwaltung der Quäker.

Logo for Quaker Relief during the Franco-Prussian War.

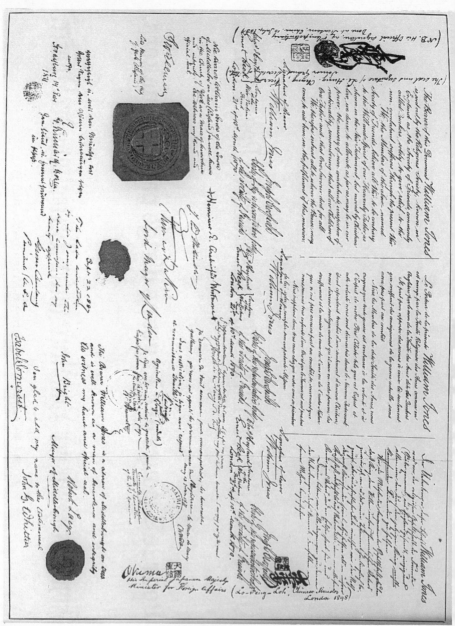

Credentials of William Jones during the Franco-Prussian War.

and coping with similar mundane matters. They all went out without special training, and often without knowing what they would do when they reached France, so improvisation was the order of the day. Many of them had private means, but those with managerial or professional work in Britain could not be absent for long. As a result, most stayed in the field for only a few weeks, often without overlapping with their successors.

ANGLO-BOER WAR

British Quakers were active during the Anglo-Boer War (1899–1902), both as proponents of peace and as providers of relief to non-combatants 'of whatever race.' Joshua Rowntree, a distinguished English Quaker and former MP, undertook an exploratory visit to South Africa and had a useful conversation with a 'thoughtful Hindu lawyer', M. K. Gandhi, about the grievances of the Indian population. Gandhi organized an Indian Ambulance Corps with no fewer than 11,000 members to work on the British side.[63]

An unusual feature of the humanitarian effort by the Friends South Africa Relief Fund Committee was the restoration of Bibles that had been taken by British soldiers from Boer households.* These Bibles had been taken before Boer homes were destroyed and the occupants herded into camps. Some 30,000 houses were destroyed in this way. Friends initiated a campaign for the return of the Bibles that had survived. Advertisements were placed in the press, and Lord Roberts (the British commander-in-chief) issued a statement to the effect that the return of the Bibles would be a kindly act which would be appreciated by 'our new fellow subjects.' By the end of 1904, 186 Bibles had been recovered, and most restored to their original owners. In addition, 3,000 Bibles in Dutch were bought from the Bible Society and distributed to the Boer clergy.

In one respect, relief work during the Anglo-Boer War broke new ground. During the Franco-Prussian War, the workers were mainly well-off people who could take off a few weeks or months from their normal lives and quickly travel the short distance to France. The

---

* I have hesitated to use the word 'looted'. James Hack Tuke, one of the Quaker workers in France during the Franco-Prussian war, gave a public lecture in the Hitchin town hall on his return. In the course of his remarks, he said: 'A little further on we came to a church, riddled with shells . . . I picked up and brought away as a relic, one of the books, which I found was a volume of the New Testament in French, dated 1796, and printed in Amsterdam. My friend also picked up a Roman Catholic mass-book.'[64]

workers in the Anglo-Boer War had to make long-term commitments to Quaker service and travel long distances.

This led to problems that had not previously been encountered. We now know that it is by no means unusual in Quaker work abroad for tension to develop between field workers and headquarters. Field workers are in direct touch with human need and tend to feel that staff and committee back home are dilatory, pedantic about procedure, and lacking in sympathy for the predicaments of workers, who often have to take quick decisions on their own responsibility. Staff and committees at home have, of course, a responsibility to financial contributors and may feel that the field workers are changing priorities or embarking on new projects without the agreement of or consultation with headquarters. Field workers may dislike the style of publicity for fundraising at home, while the people at headquarters may complain that workers in the field are failing to provide the sort of information needed to attract financial contributions. Headquarters may wish that some action be taken at once, so that the expense comes within a particular financial year, without realizing that it cannot be done 'at once' because it is the rainy season in the field or the fuel has run out.

These problems were exacerbated during the Anglo-Boer War relief by the exceptionally long time it took for written communications to travel between London and the field. There were, moreover, two additional difficulties about Anglo-Boer War relief. The first was a steadily widening difference of emphasis between those at home and those in the field. Friends at home were outraged by the conduct of the war by Britain and the suffering it was causing to innocent Boers, and also by the inflammatory tone of the jingoistic press. The field workers understood this, but they could see that there were faults on both sides in South Africa.

The second issue was whether the home committee should publish, in part or in full, frank letters and reports from field workers—an issue that has repeatedly arisen in Quaker service since then. It was argued, on the one hand, that workers overseas should report frankly on what they saw, including (if necessary) criticism of the authorities, and some Friends thought that such reports should be published at home in accordance with the commitment of Friends to truth and in the hope of influencing public opinion and public policy. Others considered that publicity of this kind would add to the difficulties of workers in the field in dealing with the authorities and would discourage them from reporting fully and honestly in the future. Moreover, the reports from one worker were sometimes contradicted by reports from another worker in a different situation. In the case of the Anglo-Boer War, the letters and reports were not published, but the secretary of the committee was authorized to disclose 'a general notification of important matters'!

FIRST WORLD WAR

During the first world war, three British Quaker or Quaker-related agencies for war relief were created. The United States entered the war on 16 April 1917, and a fortnight later, a body calling itself the Friends National Service Committee was created. On 11 May, it changed its name to the American Friends Service Committee, by which name it is still known. AFSC workers cooperated with their British and Irish counterparts in France and Russia. The Friends War Victims Relief Committee was established following a decision of Meeting for Sufferings on 4 September 1914 'to give medical and ambulance help to the non-combatants in France and Belgium.'[65] In the event, the Committee undertook refugee work in France, the Netherlands, Serbia, and Russia, and it also undertook post-war relief in Austria and Poland. Over 300 men and 150 women served abroad with the Committee during the war, joined after 1917 by some 200 Americans. John William Graham estimates that some 200 British men were exempted from military service because they were working with the War Victims Relief Committee. Not all the workers were Quakers. Most served as unpaid volunteers though a few received financial help. As in the case of relief during the Anglo-Boer War, communication between headquarters and the field was often difficult: one worker in Russia was without news from London for sixteen months. Workers in Russia were often short of money, though all were advised to hide sufficient funds to get them to the frontier in case of need.[66]

There was often tension between the British and US field workers after 1917. Many of the British had been in France for two years and had got used to spartan war-time conditions. The Americans complained of noise, squalor, and lack of decent baths and lavatories. American workers were disturbed by the aristocratic demeanour of some of their English colleagues, who seemed temperamentally incapable of fraternizing with the locally-recruited cook in France. In Russia, the vigorous Americans arrived with modern social work

War Vics clothing distribution in Russia during the first world war.

methods, such as case sheets and card indexes, and were soon im-
patient with the old-fashioned style of their British colleagues. The
British had focussed their work on the care of needy individuals: the
Americans believed that, with limited resources, it was essential to be
unsentimental and systematic. In addition, there were differences of
national temperament and, sometimes, of theology.

The intention was that aid should be given on a non-discriminatory
basis. Ruth Fry, the secretary of the Committee, insisted that the help
should take no account of the opinions of those in need: the work arose
from 'a sympathy for suffering people, and not for their Government.'
This was particularly important in Russia after the Communist revolution. Richenda Scott reports that in Russia, the peasants thought that
the only cure for sickness lay in a bottle of medicine, 'the darker and
richer in colour the better.' Rather than improve their diet or living
conditions, those who were ill thought that a short cut to better health
was to bring a present, 'to melt the heart of the nurse' so she would
produce 'the magic bottle.' The workers were often hampered by ignorance of the local language. The work was, in the main, a mere palliative: the aim, according to Ruth Fry, was to withdraw 'at the earliest
possible moment.'

The second Quaker agency for war relief was the Emergency Committee for the Assistance of Germans, Austrians, Hungarians, and
Turks in Distress (that is to say, enemy aliens), set up by Meeting for
Sufferings on 7 August 1914, three days after Britain entered the war. It
was an official Quaker body, but more than half of the Committee
members were not Friends and not all the volunteer workers were
Friends. It was concerned for the care of interned enemy civilians,
including those in a large camp on the Isle of Man, where my wife
Brenda's father was interned, and for the wives and children of interned men. The Committee encountered a certain amount of public hostility, especially during the first couple of years, on the ground that it
was unreasonable to give aid and comfort to the nation's enemies: the
writer of one letter threatened to shoot the secretary of the Committee
on sight. The Committee was able to cooperate with a similar committee in Germany, whose honorary secretary, Dr Elizabeth Rotten, later
became a Friend. After the armistice, the British Committee was amal-
gamated with the War Victims Relief Committee, which in 1924
became part of the Council for International Service.[67]

The third agency for war relief during the first world war was the

Friends Ambulance Unit. It was not part of the official machinery of London Yearly Meeting, and from time to time there was tension between the FAU and official Quaker bodies because the FAU had to cooperate closely with the military authorities. In spite of some uneasiness, Yearly Meeting in 1916 cordially endorsed a proposal 'that some Friend or Friends should convey our desire for their welfare and give them whatever spiritual help and encouragement is possible.'[68]

The initiative for the formation of the FAU came from Allan and Philip Baker (some years after Philip's marriage to Irene Noel in 1915, he became Noel-Baker), and it was the first agency associated with the Society of Friends, even if the connexion was a little tenuous, which deliberately sought to aid combatants, though it also did humanitarian work for civilians at home and abroad. Some 70% of the members were Quakers: according to the official history of the FAU, most of the original members were university and professional men. It worked closely with the military in France and Belgium, and on hospital ships in the Channel and the Mediterranean,* and two of its adjutants (Leslie Maxwell and Humphrey Nockolds) accepted honorary captaincies in the British army. One member was awarded the Distinguished Service Order, two received the Order of the British Empire, and three nurses received the Military Medal. At the end of the war, 640 members were serving abroad, 440 others in the general service section were doing work of national importance at home (mainly educational, welfare, or agricultural work), and 300 were working in hospitals.[69]

When it became clear that military conscription was inevitable, Yearly Meeting set up a Friends Service *Committee* (not to be confused with the later Friends Service *Council*) which advised Quaker men to claim unconditional exemption from military service. Many mainstream Quakers increasingly saw the FAU as easing the task of the authorities in enforcing a policy that Friends considered to be immoral, and reports began to circulate that members of the FAU in France drank wine and flirted with nurses. There was also uneasiness that those in the general service section had undertaken not to conduct anti-war propaganda. Those serving with the FAU were automatically exempt from military service and did not have to go before tribunals, although a few (like Corder Catchpool) resigned from the FAU when conscription was introduced. Corder Catchpool returned from France

* The FAU withdrew from one hospital ship because it carried troops and munitions when not carrying patients, and also German POWs as hostages.

but declined to register for military service, was arrested, refused to obey military orders, and was courtmartialed and imprisoned four times. At his fourth court-martial, he wore the Mons Ribbon which he had received from the War Office in recognition of his FAU service in France.

SECOND WORLD WAR

I now come to events of which I have personal experience or of which I have heard from family and friends. When war broke out in 1939, there was in existence the standing British and Irish Quaker agency for service abroad (the Friends Service Council) and one temporary agency for the care of the victims of the Nazi regime (the German Emergency Committee): during the course of the war, two additional relief agencies were established (the Friends Ambulance Unit and the body that was eventually known as the Friends Relief Service).

The Friends Service Council (FSC) had been set up by the merger of the Council for International Service and the Friends Foreign Mission Association. The main war relief of FSC was concerned with the care of Spanish refugees in France, and Polish and Czechoslovak refugees (including Jews) who had escaped from Nazi Germany to Hungary and Romania. This work had to be terminated in May 1940, but some of the Polish refugees eventually reached Cyprus and then Palestine, and others (mainly women and children) made their way to Tanganyika. The work for Spanish refugees in France was in due course taken over by *Secours Quaker* (under the auspices of French Friends), and the work for Polish refugees was merged in the newly-formed Friends Relief Service in 1943.[70]

The German Emergency Committee was established in 1933 to help Jews and other victims of Nazi oppression. In 1942, the name was changed to the Friends Committee for Refugees and Aliens. The German Emergency Committee staff in London came under the Friends Service Council, and after 1935, British workers in Germany were under FSC administration. The initial staff in 1933 consisted of Bertha Bracey and one assistant, but by 1939, the staff (including part-timers) numbered 119. In 1950, the Committee's remaining functions were formally transferred to FSC.[71]

The Committee began as an agency to assist those who, for religious, ethnic, or political reasons, were being persecuted by the Nazis. A Rest Home was opened in part of the Frankfurter Hof in Falkenstein in

1933, and then in St Joseph's Haus in Bad Pyrmont in 1934: these Homes provided rest and recuperation for the victims of Nazi oppression. The Bad Pyrmont Home had to close in 1939, but re-opened after the war.

Friends made representations to the German authorities in the hope of ameliorating the situation of persons of Jewish ancestry and other Nazi victims. Gilbert MacMaster, an American Friend, was able to visit one concentration camp in 1933, and William Hughes and Corder Catchpool were able to pay supervised visits to other camps in 1934–35. In 1935, Hughes wrote to Hans Thomsen, one of Hitler's legal advisors, drawing attention to a number of abuses of political prisoners by the Gestapo. He noted that 'the excesses of the earlier days were no longer taking place', but he said that 'methods of brutality' were still being used in certain places. Hughes (like Corder Catchpool) made it clear that he did not disseminate such information in Britain, and he had no wish to interfere in the internal affairs of another country. But action by the Nazi authorities to mitigate the conditions of political prisoners would have a very positive influence on international opinion.[72]

A few weeks later, Meeting for Sufferings issued an appeal to Hitler and the German people. The statement referred to 'some peculiar difficulties' in the way of deeper friendship between Germany and other countries, namely, the operation of concentration camps and other oppressive acts. Surely the time had come to abandon such drastic measures. To retain them would lay up 'an evil store of reactions, while to abandon them would awaken a response of goodwill in thousands of hearts and make for peace in the world at large.'[73]

Refugees from the Nazis were helped in France, Czechoslovakia, Austria, and other parts of the continent, and a school for refugee children was opened in the Netherlands. A major part of the work increasingly concerned the care and resettlement of Jewish refugees and, after the outbreak of war in 1939, the welfare of aliens in Britain.

When Friends work in countries with oppressive regimes, they have to take care that they do not expose others to unnecessary risks. This especially applies when crossing frontiers with lists of contacts or carrying letters. Elizabeth Fox Howard recorded an incident that happened to her when travelling home from Nazi Germany in 1935. When leaving the Quaker centre in Berlin, Corder Catchpool had handed her 'three or four letters' to be delivered to Friends House in London. She also carried a letter from William Hughes, a sealed letter from a German friend to his son informing him of the birth of the latter's son in a women's prison, her own address book listing her German contacts, and 'various secret publications issued by the Confessional Church.' She was detained at the frontier and taken to the Gestapo headquarters in Berlin. During the course of the journey, she slipped the sealed letter from the German friend down the neck of her dress and later tore it into little pieces. These were later discovered by the Gestapo and the letter was reconstructed. She was then asked who had given her the letter, but she refused to answer. She was finally released, but not all her papers were returned. She later learned that Corder Catchpool had been summoned to Gestapo headquarters for questioning, where he had been told to warn William Hughes not to come to Germany again. 'If he does, he will at once be arrested and tried.' Hughes left Berlin the next day.

The first agency specifically for war relief to be created during the war came as a result of a reunion of members of the Friends Ambulance Unit from the first world war, held at Friends House on 28 October 1938, a month after the Munich agreement. War clouds were gathering, and there was talk in Britain of introducing compulsory military service. The FAU reunion established a committee to consider whether the FAU should be reconstituted, and the following July, a few weeks after military conscription had become law, Paul Cadbury and John Harvey discussed with the Minister of Labour the CO issue and the need for alternative service. On 1 September 1939, the day the Nazis invaded Poland, *The Friend* carried a long letter from Cadbury and Harvey proposing that those who were claiming exemption from military service on conscientious grounds should undertake 'a period of constructive labour' under civilian control. If war should come, 'such a scheme could be rapidly developed to train men for relief and ambulance work.' Britain entered the war two days later. By the end of the month, the first FAU training camp assembled at Manor Farm, Birmingham, the men living in cow-sheds and eating in the barn. During the following six years, some 5,000 men applied to join the FAU, of whom 1,217 were accepted. Seventeen members lost their lives, including my two room-mates in Qujing (Kutsing), China, John Briggs and Douglas Hardy. A separate Women's FAU was started in January 1941 and merged with the other FAU later in the year. Ninety-seven women served in the FAU between 1941 and 1945. In 1942, the home section of the FAU merged with the Friends War Victims Relief Committee to form the Friends War Relief Service. The FAU formally closed down on 30 June 1946, but was succeeded by the FAU Post-War Service, which later became the FAU International Service until its termination in 1959. The FAU work in China and India was carried on after the war by the American Friends Service Committee.[74]

Those who stand firm as conscientious objectors in time of war clearly have strong convictions. It was sometimes difficult to maintain reasonable order and discipline in the FAU, and there were episodes of near anarchy. I was the leader of a small section that went out to China in 1941. We had all been issued with khaki uniform, but we contrived that no two of us ever dressed identically. Most members did their best to work as a team, but there were no sanctions except expulsion for those who would not or could not cooperate. I recall one gifted colleague, of whom I was fond, who flatly refused to take his turn at cleaning one of our hostels because he found the operation 'distasteful'.

The constitution of the FAU was complex. It was not organizationally part of the Society of Friends but all its members were supposed to 'share Quaker views on peace and war', and it reported to Yearly Meeting. For legal purposes, the self-constituted Council was the governing body. In 1940, members of the FAU began to hold staff meetings in the various sections, and the London Staff Meeting (consisting of heads of sections and senior staff at headquarters) acquired the right to nominate seven members of an Executive Committee, who were then appointed by the chairman of the Council, Paul Cadbury. After a *contretemps* in 1941 over whether a mildly erotic article could be published in the FAU *Chronicle*, an elected Advisory Committee was created to act as a kind of loyal opposition.

The first FAU had concentrated its work in Western Europe, but the second FAU was widely dispersed, with overseas sections as follows:

Europe: Austria, Belgium, Finland, Germany, Greece, Italy, the Netherlands, Norway, and Yugoslavia.

Africa and the Middle East: Egypt, Ethiopia, Lebanon, Libya, Syria, and Tunisia.

Asia: (in cooperation with the American Friends Service Committee): China and India.

At home we worked in air raid shelters in London and the provinces, ran rest centres (schools used as temporary accommodation for bombed-out families), acted as guinea-pigs for medical research, and worked as orderlies in over 80 hospitals. The hospital at Gloucester, where we initially had many difficulties, had particularly attractive nurses and provided several FAU wives.

My impression is that the FAU was not as intimately involved with the armed forces in the second world war as it had been in the first. We wore khaki uniform when in war zones and (in China, at any rate) were issued with Red Cross brassards and Red Cross badges for our forage caps. But so far as I know, no member of the reconstituted FAU in the second war accepted an honorary commission in the armed forces of Britain or its allies, and I heard of no case of an FAU member accepting a British honour or decoration for war service.

Relations with official Quaker organs were not as difficult as during the first world war. The whole of British society was mobilized for victory, so the argument about supporting or cooperating with the war effort was less potent than in 1914–18. The FAU did not automatically accept men who were exempted from military service by tribunals on condition that they joined the FAU. We took care to make clear our civilian status in war zones and to distinguish ourselves from the armed forces. When we reached China at the end of 1941, we found that it was illegal for trucks to travel empty. As much of our work consisted of taking loads of medical supplies to front-line areas, the issue arose as to what we should carry as return cargoes. It was naturally agreed that we would not carry munitions or soldiers being redeployed, but that we had no objection to carrying civilian persons or supplies, or wounded combatants in need of medical care. The difficult moral issue concerned dual-purpose items: tungsten, which could be used for light bulb filaments or electronic tubes for military purposes; mercury, which could be used for medical thermometers or in barometers for military aircraft; pig bristles, which could be used for making domestic brushes or camouflage netting. To carry these cargoes was highly lucrative, and we were often short of money. In the end, the policy adopted (if it can be called a policy) was to leave it to the conscience of each individual FAU member to decide whether to carry any particular ambiguous item.[75] In 1944, the China Unit received a request from the military to use our trucks to rush reinforcements to meet a dangerous Japanese offensive in the Guiyang (Kweiyang) area: naturally the request was refused.[76]

The Friends War Victims Relief Committee was established on 1

Dr Robert McClure (FAU, China) operating on a patient in Baoshan (Paoshan), in the Salween Front, West China.

November 1940, fourteen months after the formation of the FAU.[77] In 1942, the War Victims Relief Committee merged with the home relief section of the FAU to form the Friends War Relief Service. This newly merged body was later reorganized to form the Friends Relief Service (by which name I will now call it). In 1948, FRS handed over its remaining work to the Friends Service Council, one of the predecessors of Quaker Peace and Service. By the time of closure of FRS in 1948, it had had 1,232 members, the balance between the sexes being much more equal than it had been in the FAU: 629 men and 603 women.[78]

Until the end of the war in Europe, FRS concentrated on civilian relief at home. It engaged in welfare work in air raid shelters and rest centres in London and the provinces, worked in clubs and settlements, helped in Citizens Advice Bureaux, and ran hostels for those evacuated from London and other bombed or vulnerable cities.

In the last few months of the war, several teams began work overseas. Two members had gone to Morocco to help in the care of European refugees, but their third report read, 'No work, no letters, no trunks, no money'; two members went to Italy to care for displaced persons and refugees; a team arrived in Greek islands in the Aegean in March 1945 to help settle refugees; in April, a team was called to the Belsen concentration camp to help with the care and repatriation of surviving inmates; and there were other scattered pieces of work abroad that had been started by local initiative and then brought within FRS or FSC auspices.

There was, perhaps, a certain irony about the status within Quakerdom of the two relief agencies. As noted above, the FAU had no formal connexion with official organs of London Yearly Meeting, but all its members were pacifists who shared Quaker views on peace and war. The body that eventually became the Friends Relief Service was never wholly pacifist and only about 40% Quaker. The purposes of the two agencies differed. The FAU was established to provide a civilian alternative to military conscription: the purpose of the FRS was not to find work but, in the words of its general secretary and historian, for 'the relief of civilian distress.'

Relations between the FAU and the FRS were not always easy. Roger Wilson, the general secretary of FRS, found that the FAU 'moved with much self-assurance and limited humility.' The 'very able and decisive' members of the FAU 'were sometimes painfully direct in their criticism of what they judged to be the muddled and inefficient administration of the work inherited from the War Vics stream, while those drawn from the latter tradition were more than a little critical of what they judged to be the kick and rush tendencies of the Unit'. The FAU's 'strongest point', according to Wilson, 'was its complete ignorance of history. There was a sort of divine innocence which enabled it to act with certainty.'

Like the FAU, FRS struggled to combine Quakerly concern, efficient leadership, and a reasonable degree of democratic decision-making. The challenge was to reconcile the wisdom and experience of weighty Friends with the enthusiasm and knowledge of those actually doing the work, some of whom manifested 'the streak of anarchy which often appears in the young and immature conscientious objector.' There was also the usual problem of failures of communication and understanding between headquarters and the field.

The question of uniform for FRS proved very difficult to resolve. When the sending of FRS teams overseas arose in 1944, the War Office insisted that civilian workers in military areas should wear uniform: FAU members in war zones overseas had worn khaki, often with Red Cross insignia, but FRS members were divided on whether it was appropriate for civilians doing relief work under official Quaker auspices to be almost indistinguishable in appearance from members of the armed forces. The matter was discussed at Yearly Meeting in 1944. In my experience, Yearly Meeting cannot easily reach a decision when its subordinate bodies are divided. Certainly the discussion in 1944 was confused and sometimes incoherent. Roger Wilson subsequently described it as 'most unhappy, stimulating more heat than light . . . A Yearly Meeting of 700 or 800 people on a hot afternoon, gathered under the shadow of the great military assault on Europe, was not a good place in which to consider such an issue.' The Yearly Meeting minute read in part:

> The wearing of khaki uniform by our members . . . is felt by many Friends to symbolize a closer collaboration with the military than we should support as a Society. We therefore ask Friends Relief Service . . . not to send out parties in khaki uniform in the name of the Society of Friends; but either to wait until uniform of another distinctive colour is available, or to second to other organizations those of their workers who are concerned for this work.
> This meeting is far from easy in the situation thus created . . . [79]

Shortly after this, the War Office agreed to a uniform of Quaker grey for FRS. This episode had its absurd side, for when one of the first FRS units to go abroad reached the Aegean, it found that the islands were occupied by Indian troops in grey uniform, so the team switched to khaki.

> There was no moment of a collective decision to move into khaki [John Saunders writes], but rather a practical and piecemeal adoption of the measure . . . For one thing there was no regular supply of even bits of ex-army uniform on the local market . . . As I recall, the reaction of individual team members was simply to obtain a second-hand battle dress khaki blouse as and when possible . . . I wore khaki because all my clothing had been lost when I was shipwrecked on 3 May 1945, travelling from Athens to the Aegean. The British army quartermaster in Athens kindly replaced what I had lost but of course out of military issue.[80]

Another issue for FRS, perhaps of greater moral substance, arose in occupied Germany, when General Montgomery issued an order prohibiting 'fraternization' between allied troops or civilian teams with the Germans. FRS decided to withdraw the teams that were standing by to work in Germany. Finally, FRS decided that it was useless to argue about the matter with the War Office in a formal way: FRS, if allowed into occupied Germany, 'should be free as persons to treat other people as persons and not as units in prescribed categories.' In due course, FRS teams entered Germany and treated the German population as human beings.

SOME PROCESSES AND PREDICAMENTS OF QUAKER WAR RELIEF

Quaker service is not simply what is organized in and from Friends House in London, but service by Quakers: in the family, for the Meeting, at work, in the locality. For more than two centuries, there was no standing machinery in London Yearly Meeting for relief abroad, but individual Friends, acting under concern, collected funds for relief, and often went to the areas of need to engage in or supervise the work.

With the development of modern means of communication, Friends heard more quickly and more vividly of a war, a flood, or a famine while it was actually occurring or soon thereafter. During the Franco-Prussian War (1870–1), a Friends War Relief Fund was created, with one paid employee in London, most of the overseas workers being persons of means who paid their own expenses and went to France for a few weeks or, at most, three months. (Roger Wilson commented in his Swarthmore Lecture that Friends 'tend not to find themselves among the economically insecure'[81]). By the standards of today, the operation was not at all professional.

The situation was different during the Anglo-Boer War (1899–1902). Distances were much greater, means of communication more difficult, and Britain was a belligerent. Some of the problems that were to arise in later war relief began to be manifested during this period—different emphases and sympathies between headquarters and the field, problems over the publication in Britain of letters and reports, and so on. Field workers could see with their own eyes what was happening, while the home committee relied on reports in the newspapers and the views of ardent anti-war campaigners like Emily Hobhouse.

Official Quaker agencies have usually stipulated that relief shall be given to non-combatants. This has been because of the difficulty for pacifists of operating in a war zone without being subject to unacceptable military restrictions, and the belief that giving humanitarian aid to a wounded soldier facilitates his return to the fighting front in order to carry on the war. The Friends Ambulance Units in the two world wars, not being officially sponsored by London Yearly Meeting, were able to make it a matter of policy to help all in need, civilian or combatant, allied or enemy, oppressor or oppressed. This occasionally placed the FAU in battle areas where the choice was between compromising principles or withdrawing personnel.

The basic principle of Quaker work is that help is given without adverse discrimination—what the International Committee of the Red Cross calls 'the principle of neutrality'. Clarence Pickett of AFSC described a situation in Austria after the unsuccessful *putsch* in 1934, when the Vienna Centre was asked to give food to the families of imprisoned Nazis. Pickett himself had reservations about meeting the request, but Rufus Jones had 'a real sense of vigorous concern that we should not let our objection to the prisoners' Nazi views prevent our taking care of their families if it was humanly possible.' Duncan Wood has pointed out that many German children who were fed by the Quakers after the first world war must have lived long enough to help the invading Nazi armies.[82] Yet we must give assistance where it is needed, and we cannot control the future actions of those we help.

In situations of acute need and when food is desperately short, relief workers inevitably feel uneasy if they are adequately fed while those they are there to help are starving. Jack Catchpool described a situation in Moscow during the first world war when a YMCA team arrived from Siberia with a small consignment of food. Catchpool had not seen food like this for months: 'It was a magnificent treat for me to have my meals [with the YMCA team] although I felt somewhat ashamed at the thought of all the people who were going without.'[83]

When food is short, the natural instinct of the relief worker is to feed the most vulnerable people: children, old people, the sick. But circumstances have occurred, as in Russia during the first world war, when it was arguably more rational, and in the long run more humane, to give priority to those who would plant next year's crops and bear the next generation of children.

In addition to the war relief referred to in the previous pages, British Quaker agencies have provided relief for the victims of many wars since 1945: Palestine and Israel, China, Korea, Hungary, Algeria, the Congo (Zaire), Vietnam, Nigeria-Biafra, El Salvador-Honduras, Sri Lanka, and Iraq, among others.

The present set-up for Quaker service in London Yearly Meeting comprises three elements: committees, headquarters staff, and overseas workers. Those who comprise these three entities are likely to have different qualifications and have had varied past experiences. Committees will include Friends with substantial experience of the region or function concerned, but experience of *what it used to be like* when they lived there or worked on that function. Their views of what is important may differ from those of headquarters staff or field workers. Fixing priorities is one of the hardest tasks that a Quaker committee faces. Henry van Etten, the distinguished French Quaker, suggested twenty-four principles for Quaker work, of which one read:

> One must be able to withdraw without flourish or show when a successfully initiated action can be taken up and continued by others, even outside the Society of Friends.[84]

It is difficult to lay down old work, and especially so when there are Friends who are strongly attached to it. There is, however, a good Quaker tradition of pioneering new work in an adventurous spirit, and then handing it over to others when it is firmly rooted or has become more generally acceptable.

The committees of the Quaker agencies operate on usual Quaker principles, seeking the will of God and reaching decisions without voting. Clarence Pickett, on the basis of twenty-two years experience as executive secretary of the AFSC, wrote:

> The ideal of AFSC, in line with Quaker practice, is that decisions on matters small and great should be made on the basis of unanimity . . . Usually if a group will go deep enough it can find ground acceptable to all . . . In this, as in all else, we do not attain to perfection, but . . . I have never known a deep and continuing dissension. Many times wide differences of opinion have existed, but in the end usually something better than anyone had at first conceived becomes the basis of action.[85]

The headquarters staff will be expected to have a good deal of knowledge and vision about the region or function within their sphere of responsibility. They will soon learn about administrative procedures at Friends House, methods of appointing and training workers, the importance of accurate budgeting and accounting, how to respond constructively to reports from the field, the needs of publicity, and so on. In time, they may acquire more current information than have the members of the committees they serve, but they must be constantly on guard not to supplant the policy-making functions of committees, and not to respond unsympathetically to requests and complaints from the sometimes inexperienced field workers.

Cooperation between British and US Quaker agencies has not always been easy, especially when work has been undertaken in parallel. Difficulties were encountered in both France and Russia during the closing stages of the first world war, and—to come to more recent times—in attitudes and policies regarding Southern Africa in the 1970s. But on the whole, cooperation has worked well when there has been adequate consultation before the work begins. It has been found by experience that joint *sponsorship* of work by several Quaker agencies is often desirable, but that *administration* should be in the hands of one agency only.

Since the second world war and the post-war emergency, there have been nearly two hundred wars, mostly in the Southern hemisphere, so most Quaker war relief has been directed to what Dag Hammarskjold called the Third World (to distinguish it from the Old World and the

New World).* Relief workers from Western Quaker agencies need to take special care not to harbour feelings of superiority or arrogance. Quakers happen to have originated, and largely to have spread, in fortunate parts of the world, normally free of natural disasters, with temperate climates, and blessed with abundant natural resources. Quaker workers may sometimes be dismayed at bribery in the countries in which they work, forgetting that corruption and nepotism were normal in Britain before 1853 and that there are few days now when our media do not report major cases of embezzlement and fraud in our own countries. Colonialism was not wholly bad, but it fostered attitudes of cultural arrogance and condescension on the part of the colonizer and dependence, apathy, and irresponsibility on the part of the colonized. Developing countries face massive problems and are trying to achieve in one or two generations the developments that were spread over centuries in the West.

Workers engaged in war relief are at the end of a long administrative chain. They are likely to be in unfamiliar and sometimes dangerous situations, eating strange food, sleeping on uncomfortable beds, suffering from recurrent attacks of diarrhoea, speaking the local language inadequately, lonely, receiving instructions from headquarters that are irrelevant or impossible of fulfilment, and doing work that is boring or seems futile. They may resent the local mores over such matters as administrative style, nepotism and corruption, or sexual conduct. They may face difficult choices over visa requirements and work permits, whether to change foreign currency at official or unofficial rates, and how to handle abuses of human rights that come to their attention. They may find that relief supplies are not distributed on the basis of need but at the whim of corrupt officials, local war-lords, or camp mafias.

There are times when field workers feel that they have been forgotten by headquarters. One conscientious worker for war refugees told me that headquarters never commented on her written reports. She quoted to me the lines of Longfellow:

I shot an arrow into the air,
It fell to earth, I knew not where.

* 'The following day [September 1960], U Thant called on Hammarskjold. During the conversation, Hammarskjold suggested that perhaps the Afro-Asian Group, with like-minded countries in Latin America, should adopt the name "Third World". "After all," he said, "we already have the Old and the New Worlds, why not the Third World?" '[86]

Field workers sometimes dislike the publicity of the home base for fund-raising purposes, and headquarters staff and committees sometimes object to local publicity in the field. During the Nazi times, an AFSC mission to Germany led by Rufus Jones was ridiculed in the press in both Germany and the United States, and the Quaker refugee work in the Gaza Strip after the 1948 Palestine war received what Clarence Pickett described as 'a consistently bad press in Egypt.'[87]

In situations of crisis following war or disaster, the host government may be in a chaotic condition and unable to cope coherently with foreign relief agencies. Francesca Wilson, writing of the situation in Serbia after the first world war, had this to say.

> There were dozens of different organisations struggling for a foothold. The new constituted Government . . . had enough on its hands without having to be polite to all sorts of foreigners who importuned it for buildings, transport, personnel, priority and privilege. Ministers of Departments could not tell who was important and did not like to be rude to earnest Anglo-Saxons, who had left their own countries, ostensibly at great sacrifice and with the most benevolent intentions, and who dangled before their eyes all sorts of benefits for widows and orphans, for the diseased and maimed and blind. As a rule, they promised the same building to half-a-dozen different people and gave it to none of them. Heads of missions were frantic over unimplemented promises and unanswered requests.[88]

Quaker service agencies do not wish for military protection when working in war-zones. In the FAU in China during the second world war, we took care to distinguish ourselves from those agencies that were said to misuse the Red Cross emblem by mixing civilian and military vehicles in relief convoys. On 6 May 1948, nine days before the Arab states went to war against Israel, Harold Evans was appointed Special Municipal Commissioner for Jerusalem. Evans was chair of the Board of the AFSC, and he was appointed because a Quaker was acceptable to both Arabs and Jews. He got as far as Cairo, but never reached Jerusalem because he was unwilling to accept the protection of a military escort.[89] In 1992, the UN Security Council authorized the use of force to protect humanitarian aid in Bosnia-Herzegovina and Somalia: I doubt whether QPS would accept military protection, even if that were the only way of getting life-saving supplies to war victims.

There have been times in the past when British Friends, like some of the Old Testament prophets, have regarded misfortune or disaster as God's punishments for human misdeeds. During the middle of the famine in Ireland due to a potato blight (1845–49), London Yearly Meeting's epistle claimed that God had been 'pleased' to impose a sore affliction on the people of Ireland in the hope that they would benefit from the divine chastening and that it would sanctify them in this life and the life to come.

> Within the last year, it has pleased the Almighty to visit the nation of Ireland with sore affliction . . . it may be, that in the sufferings which he has permitted to befal some of his children, he designs not only to bless his chastening to their greatest benefit, both in this life and that which is to come, but to sanctify it to those that are round them.[90]

I hope that modern Friends would not be guilty of such implausible sanctimony.

War relief is necessarily a palliative, a necessary response to an emergency, but leaving the malady uncured. Henry van Etten, in the article already referred to, stated as another principle of Quaker relief that it should attempt to attack the causes of evil and not to be content with improving unsatisfactory conditions.[91] To make war relief unnecessary means working to remove the causes of war, to achieve respect for human rights, to help the parties to resolve conflict peacefully. War relief is never enough: Friends also have a vocation to build a just and peaceful world.

3

QUAKER PEACE-MAKING

III. QUAKER PEACE-MAKING

I suggested earlier that, over the centuries, the image of Friends had changed from dangerous rebels to respectable rebels. One reason for this was that our refusal to fight has been complemented by humanitarian service for war victims. Another reason is that we have taken seriously the obligation to build a peaceful world by such means as support for international agencies to promote peace and justice, the advocacy of disarmament and methods to resolve disputes by peaceful means, the promotion of peace and conflict research, the exercise of mediation and good offices, and the raising of public awareness about underlying issues of peace and war.

ADVICE TO RULERS

Friends have never been diffident about offering advice to rulers about how to achieve peace. I would like to take four examples from different centuries to show how the content of what Friends have said has changed. Robert Barclay's *Epistle of Love and Friendly Advice* seems to have been a personal initiative, addressed to the ambassadors gathered at Nijmegen in 1678 to negotiate the ending of the war between France and the Netherlands. Barclay does not concern himself with the territorial and financial issues separating the belligerents, but with what he calls 'The chief ground, cause and root' of all the misery afflicting Christians, that is to say, that they are Christians in name only and not in nature. This is 'especially manifest in the clergy . . . who for the most part are the greatest promoters . . . of wars.' Although the rulers then at variance may be brought to lay down their arms and may appear to be good friends and allies, this situation will not last 'unless the Lord Jesus Christ can be restored to his kingdom in their hearts . . .' Only by the light of Christ can the rulers be led out of the darkness, strife, and the lusts from which wars come, and into the ways of righteousness and peace, which leads people not to destroy but to love and forgive. The letter in Latin, together with copies of Barclay's *Apology*, were handed to the ambassadors at Nijmegen on 23 and 24 February 1678. I have not been able to discover how Barclay's writings were received.

Seventy years later, the exercise was repeated for the benefit of the delegates gathered at Aix-la-Chapelle (Aachen) to negotiate an end to the War of the Austrian Succession. This time the decision was taken by Meeting for Sufferings. Seventy-four copies of Barclay's *Apology* in various languages, together with an explanatory memorandum, were

And the Delivery thereof to the Embassadors

Occurrences that happened in delivering
Robert Barclay's Apologies at y Request
of the Meeting for Sufferings in
London, to the following Ambassadors
met to Conclude a General Peace at
Aix La Chapelle, in the Months
7ber & 8ber 1748. by me
Jan Vander Werf of Amsterdam.

N.S.
1748
7b: 27.

With y Imperial Ambassador Count Caunitz,
Deliverd three Books, high Dutch, One for the Emperor
One for the Empress Queen, & One for him the Ambassador,
with a Letter: He received me Kindly, & having
Read the Letter & Title of the Book, he asked on
what Occasion I brought him them? and having
answered him, he asked further if I had the Books
in Other Languages, I answered, Yes; He asked then if
I had been or intended to go to any other of the Ambassa-
:dors? I answered, I intended to go to the other Ambassa-
:dors; tho' had not yet been: He then desired one in
French, if I could Spare one, which I promised, & Sent
him in the Afternoon One Book French; He asked
the Bearer if I had been with any other Ambassador;
and being answer'd Yes, with the Ambassadors Sandwich,
and S' Severin, tho' the Porter of the Last, being a Switzer,
Refused me Admittance: to which the Ambassador
said, I should try again to morrow morning
Clapping the Messenger on the Shoulder.

Ditto.   With the Ambassador of Great Britain,
Earl of Sandwich, Deliverd Two Books English,
One for him, & One for his first Secretary: and after
he had Read the Letter, he thanked me, and Said
he should do his best towards so good a Work.

28th.   With the first French Ambassador
Count S' Severin, went to him the Second time
and deliverd him the Books & Letter, he gave the
                                        Letter

Part of Jan van der Werf's report to Meeting for Sufferings on his contacts with
delegates to the peace conference at Aix-la-Chapelle, 1748.

distributed to the delegates with the help of a Dutch Friend, Jan van der Werf. The reception varied. The French ambassador, finding that the *Apology* concerned religious matters, said he did not need it. The Spanish ambassador suggested that he should pay for the book and, when that was declined, offered his visitors a cup of coffee or cocoa. The Papal Nuncio, after a considerable discussion of religious matters with his visitor, asked, 'Can Catholics be saved?' 'I cannot judge other men', replied van der Werf. The episode cost £30 in all, or about £2,500 in modern currency.[92]

My example from the nineteenth century is the Quaker mission to Tsar Nicholas in 1854 in the hope of averting the Crimean War. The moving spirit was Joseph Sturge, who raised the matter at Meeting for Sufferings in January 1854. An address to Nicholas I was approved, and Robert Charleton and Henry Pease were appointed to accompany Sturge to St Petersburg. The gist of the message was a humanitarian appeal to avoid resort to arms, and Friends were careful not to offer an opinion on the questions at issue between Russia and other states.

The three Friends travelled via Düsseldorf, Berlin, Königsberg (later called Kaliningrad) and Riga (now in Latvia), reaching St Petersburg on 2 February. (Friends were always meticulous in omitting 'St' before Petersburg!). Robert Charleton was struck by the 'strict punctuality and the capitally good arrangements' of the German trains, 'not very inferior to . . . the Great Western express.' The journey took place 'without the slightest impediment from political causes.' The three Friends lodged at Benson's Hotel and soon secured an appointment with Count Nesselrode, the Russian Chancellor, who received them 'with great courtesy and affability.' As the Tsar was unable to receive them for several days, Nesselrode arranged for the visitors to do some sightseeing, but Joseph Sturge found this distracting, for his mind was 'too ill at ease with the prospect of the visit to the Emperor . . . at which it may be so important not to say too little or too much.'[93]

The meeting with the Tsar took place on 10 February. Joseph Sturge read the message of Friends and explained the constitution of Meeting for Sufferings. The address recalled the interest in Quakerism shown by the Tsar's brother, Tsar Alexander I, during a visit to Britain in 1814. The purpose of the Quaker visitors was to appeal for peace 'as the manifest duty of a Christian Government.' 'Deeply to be deplored would it be were . . . peace [to be] exchanged for the unspeakable horrors of war.' 'The more fully the Christian is persuaded of the justice of his own cause, the greater his magnanimity in the exercise of fore-bearance.' The address concluded by expressing the hope that, in due time, the Tsar would exchange an earthly crown for a heavenly one. The Tsar replied in French, and an official version of the reply was later provided. He said that he did not desire war: 'I abhor it as sincerely as you do . . .' He wanted to avoid it by all possible means, but he could not be indifferent to the interests and honour of his country. After the formal proceedings, the Tsar invited his visitors to be seated, 'kindly giving us a full opportunity for making any verbal statement that we might wish to offer.' Joseph Sturge then proceeded to express his con-cern, 'not entering into the political matters involved in the dispute, but confining himself to the moral and religious aspects of the matter.' He emphasized that neither the Society of Friends nor a large propor-tion of right-thinking people at home approved of the inflammatory tone of the English press. Many of those who favoured a settlement of international disputes by arbitration had incurred the hostility of those who relied on physical force. If war came, the principal victims would be 'innocent men with their wives and children.' When the conver-sation was concluded, the Tsar 'with eyes moistened with emotion', shook hands 'very cordially', accompanied them to the door, and then shook their hands again. He wanted to present his visitors with small gifts of their choice as souvenirs of St Petersburg, but the three Friends thought that to accept gifts would reduce their moral influence in favour of peace when they got back home. The three of them sat up late, drafting and redrafting a reply to the Tsar that would not cause offence.[94]

Some non-Quaker peace workers were critical of this enterprise. Richard Cobden wrote to Sturge suggesting that there were more important things to do at home. Quakers were too fond of consorting with the great, and a Quaker deputation to the Tsar would expose them to the charge of seeking their own glorification.

> Nothing short of a miracle could enable such a deputation to accom-plish the end in view; and miracles are not wrought in our times.[95]

My fourth example of a Quaker approach to a head of government comes from the twentieth century and had one unusual feature in that Meeting for Sufferings had declined to recognize the Committee con-cerned as an official Quaker agency. This was the Friends League of Nations Committee, formed in July 1918, which presented an address to US President Wilson during his visit to London in 1918. The delegation was led by Joseph Albert Pease (Lord Gainford).

An attempt had been made to reconcile the views of the Committee and Meeting for Sufferings, but without success. A joint committee agreed on two points: that international disputes should be settled by conciliation or judicial procedures, and that the accumulation of armaments was contrary to the will of God. But the unofficial League of Nations Committee wanted the armaments not eliminated to be placed at the disposal of the League of Nations for enforcement action as a last resort. The Friends Peace Committee held strongly that Friends must maintain the traditional testimony against all war and against any attempt to enforce ideas by violence.[96]

There was great concern in Meeting for Sufferings at the lack of unity on the ultimate means of enforcing decisions of the League of Nations. One Friend (Metford Warner) wanted to forget about the League of Nations and unite in trying to keep Christ before the world. Another Friend (Barrow Cadbury) asked that prayers be offered for Lord Robert Cecil. The minute finally adopted noted that there was much in the statement produced by the joint committee with which all Friends would heartily agree, but that it would be a calamity if the only Christian pacifist body were to affirm publicly 'that military force is, on certain occasions, the ultimate remedy for wrong.' The minute concluded with the assurance that nothing but good could result from 'the amicable discussion of our point of difference.'[97]

The deputation that saw President Wilson was, therefore, a body claiming to represent 'a very substantial proportion of the adult membership' of London Yearly Meeting, but not speaking officially for the Society of Friends. The address praised Wilson's efforts for freedom, liberty, and peace. The Committee wanted to see a new and better set of relations between nations. States should agree to submit all differences to judicial tribunals or conciliation councils, agreeing in advance to accept their findings. International efforts were needed to end the arms race, and a solemn international compact should be agreed to use arms 'solely under the sanction of the League of Nations for the maintenance of international peace.'

This last point was treacherous ground for a British Quaker committee, but more was to follow.

We agree that goodwill and moral influence are the essential bases of a League of Nations, but we cannot exclude the possible need for the exercise of economic pressure and even, in the last resort, the use of such force as may become necessary to restrain the evildoer . . .

President Wilson responded in cordial terms.[98]

The approaches to the delegates at Nijmegen in 1678 and Aix-la-Chapelle in 1748 were straightforward appeals to take the teachings of Jesus Christ seriously. The mission to Tsar Nicholas in 1854 included that element, but it also appealed to his humanitarian sentiments. The deputation to President Wilson in 1918 advocated specific measures to achieve peace, including procedures for the peaceful settlement of disputes, disarmament, and sanctions (including military enforcement) to counter aggression.

PENN AND BELLERS

Many Friends considered that the League of Nations Committee had departed from true Quaker principles, but two early Friends had proposed that peace be maintained by collective military force. William Penn's plan for a European parliament was published exactly three hundred years ago this year. This was not an advocacy of full-blooded pacifism, and it was not published under Quaker auspices.[99] Penn listed a number of benefits of his proposal, of which the following six are the more interesting.*

1. It would prevent the spilling of much 'Human and Christian Blood.'
2. The reputation of Christianity would 'in some degree' be recovered in the sight of infidels.
3. It would save money, especially on espionage and pensions for war widows and orphans.
4. It would make travel easier and safer.
5. It would increase friendship between states and rulers.
6. Princes would be able to choose wives for love, 'and not by Proxy, merely to gratify interest; an Ignoble motive.'[100]

Penn's idea was that 'that which prevents a civil war in a nation is that which may prevent it abroad, viz., Justice.' Peace 'is maintained by justice, which is a fruit of government, as government is from society, and society from consent.' Disorder is prevented by justice, when no man is a judge in his own cause.[101]

Penn proceeded from these axioms to detailed proposals, by which

*Penn, as was the custom in those days, was lavish in his use of italics: I have used ordinary type.

AN ESSAY

Towards the Prefent and Future

PEACE

OF

Europe,

BY THE

Eftablifhment of an *European*

Dyet, Parliament,

Or Eftates.

Beati Pacifici.

Cædant Arma Togæ.

London, Printed in the Year, 1693.

W. Penn.

Title page of William Penn's plan for a European parliament, 1693.

the representatives of rulers would meet and agree to establish 'Rules of Justice'. All disputes should be submitted to this assembly for a peaceful settlement. And if any ruler should reject the judgment and delay compliance or resort to armed force, all the other rulers should unite to compel the recalcitrant ruler to abide by the collective decision. Voting would be weighted, based on what we would now call the gross domestic product of each state. There would be ninety votes in all 'if the Turks and Muscovites are taken in as seems but fit and Just'; England ('I pretend to no manner of Exactness') would have six votes.[102]

Penn gave attention to some practical details. In order to avoid quarrels about precedence, the meeting hall should be round, with several doors, so that the heads of delegation could enter simultaneously. The presidency should rotate. The official languages would be Latin and French: 'The first would be very well for Civilians, but the last most easy for Men of Quality.' Voting would be by secret ballot so as to prevent corruption: if any delegates should be so vile, false, and dishonourable as to be influenced by money, 'they have the advantage of taking their money . . . and of Voting undiscovered to the Interest of their Principals, and their own Inclination.' Decisions should be by a three-quarters majority. The records should be kept in a trunk or chest with several locks.[103]

The penultimate section dealt with possible objections.

Objection	Answer
1. The strongest and richest will never agree.	No ruler is stronger than all the rest.
2. It would lead to effeminacy from the disuse of soldiery.	Each ruler can introduce a suitable discipline in the education of youth: 'This would make them Men: Neither Women nor Lyons.'
3. There would be no employment for the younger sons of families.	Let them become merchants, farmers, or scientists.
4. Sovereign rulers will become not sovereign, a thing they will never agree to.	They will be as sovereign at home as ever they were. 'And if this be called a lessening of their Power, it must be only because the great Fish can no longer eat up the little ones.'[104]

17

SOME
REASONS
FOR AN
European State,

PROPOSED

To the POWERS of *EUROPE*,

By an Univerſal Guarantee, and an Annual
Congreſs, Senate, Dyet, or Parliament,

To Settle any Diſputes about the BOUNDS and RIGHTS
of PRINCES and STATES hereafter.

With an Abſtract of a SCHEME form'd by King *Henry* the
Fourth of *France*, upon the ſame Subject.

And alſo,

A PROPOSAL for a General Council or Convocation of all
the different Religious Perſwaſions in *Chriſtendom*, (not to
Diſpute what they Differ about, but) to Settle the General
Principles they Agree in: By which it will appear, that they
may be good Subjects and Neighbours, tho' of different Ap-
prehenſions of the Way to Heaven.

In order to prevent Broils and War at home, when foreign
Wars are ended.

*And above all things, have fervent Charity among your ſelves:
for Charity ſhall cover the multitude of Sins,* 1 Pet. 4. v. 8.

LONDON: Printed *Anno* 1710.

Title page of John Bellers' plan for a European federation, 1710.

Penn concluded on a slightly chauvinistic note. 'But I confess I have the Passion to wish heartily that the honour of Proposing and Effecting so great and good a design might be owing to England.'[105]

John Bellers wrote his plan for a European state in 1710, seventeen years after the publication of Penn's pamphlet, but Bellers added a proposal for an ecumenical assembly to deal with religious issues.[106]

Bellers was imbued with the same moral fervour as Penn. War always ruins more people than it helps, whereas peace is so precious that no sacrifice can be too great to put a stop to the useless effusion of blood. Those rulers who achieve peace in Christendom will have the assurance of eternal crowns hereafter.[107]

Alliances are constantly changing, but a federal union would endure. The assembly that Bellers proposed would consist of allies, neutrals, and enemies. The rulers would renounce all claims against each other, for their goal would be unity and not division, peace and not war. Each of the countries of Europe would choose its own form of government, and the unity of the rulers abroad would not detract from their sovereignty at home.[108]

There were several favourable references to the Grand Design of the Duc de Sully (1560–1641) and to the treatise of 'the Eminent and Accomplished Gentleman,' William Penn; but the plan which Bellers put forward takes less account of international realities than Penn's. Instead of Penn's proposal for weighted voting, Bellers proposed that Europe 'should be divided into 100 equal Cantons or Provinces . . . that every Sovereign Prince and State may send one Member to the Senate.' Like Penn, Bellers favoured the inclusion of the Muscovites and Muslims (Turks), who only need the same opportunities and mental application to be the same men: 'But to beat their Brains out, to put sense into them, is a great mistake.' The senate would meet annually, and it would proceed by argument and not by the sword. It would decide on the permitted levels of armed forces for each country, and would itself dispose of sufficient forces to prevent or defeat aggression.[109]

Bellers also proposed a general council of all Christian Churches and sects. Many wars were caused by religious animosity, he wrote, and these wars could be avoided by setting up an ecumenical council, not to dispute what they differed about but to agree on the general principles on which they could all agree. There would be one general religious council for Europe, and three subordinate regional councils.

When the council assembled, they would discover that they could be good neighbours, 'tho of different Apprehensions of the Way to Heaven.' There were two matters on which they would find agreement, love of God and love of neighbours.[110]

FRIENDS ENGAGE WITH THE WORLD'S PROBLEMS
In the century after the death of George Fox in 1691, Friends in Britain made few converts and were not greatly concerned with the world's problems. They took seriously Paul's advice in his letters to the Colossians and to Titus. Men were to be sober, grave, temperate, loving to their wives, sound in faith, in charity, and in patience. Women were to be holy, discreet, chaste, not given to much wine, submissive to their husbands and loving their children. Children were to obey their parents and servants their masters. Friends should not be ashamed to be 'a peculiar people', mainly concerned with nurturing the spiritual life of their own members: pure religion was to keep themselves 'unspotted from the world.'[111] They distrusted logic and reason, which they thought of as 'creaturely', and instead sought an inward retirement. The discipline of the Society was largely concerned with simplicity of living: plain speech and dress, the disowning of those who married non-Friends, the rejection of aesthetic pleasure. During the century of Quaker introspection after the death of George Fox, membership of London Yearly Meeting dropped by more than half (from around 50,000 in 1691 to less than 20,000 a century later).

It is not clear to me what were the factors that caused Friends to emerge from this period of isolation, of spiritual inwardness, of relative unconcern with the world's problems. It may have been that the Age of Enlightenment began to have an effect on Friends, an understanding that the Inner Light was not confined to the development of spiritual life but could lead to concern for the affairs of the secular world, a belief in human progress based on universal rational principles. But whether or not that was the case, the fact remains that British Friends emerged from their period of introspection and withdrawal around 1790. Perhaps a harbinger of this new mood of engagement was London Yearly Meeting's petition against slavery in 1783, made at the suggestion of Philadelphia Friends. Friends appealed to Parliament to heed the suffering of enslaved Negroes and place a total ban on the slave trade. The following year, Meeting for Sufferings prepared 'a small Tract' on the evils of slavery, to be published 'in an extensive manner.' Yearly Meeting decided that the few Friends who were not wholly clear of involvement in the slave trade should be 'laboured with in a Spirit of Love and Meekness.'[112]

From the 1790s on, Friends began to cooperate with other Christians over other social issues such as the care of the mentally ill, the relief of poverty, improvement of working conditions, the provision of free schools, prison reform, temperance, and world peace.

Friends, including William Allen and Joseph Tregelles Price, were active in forming a Peace society in 1816. Its basis was that 'war is inconsistent with the spirit of Christianity and the true instincts of mankind.' Its programme included goals which non-Quakers could share, such as the reduction of armaments and agreed mechanisms for the peaceful settlement of disputes.[113]

An important articulation of the more outward-looking attitude of Friends came in the 1820s in the writings of the young Jonathan Dymond—he died at the age of 32. Dymond followed Barclay in basing his rejection of war on both scriptural and prudential grounds, but he sought to enlist non-Quaker pacifists and even non-pacifists in the effort to prevent war.

Friends were active in the organizing of international non-governmental peace conferences. The idea had originated with Elihu Burritt, a blacksmith from Connecticut. Conferences were held in Brussels in 1848, Paris in 1849 (presided over by Victor Hugo), Frankfurt in 1850, London in 1851 (held in Exeter Hall in the Strand, demolished in 1907, the site now being graced by the Strand Palace Hotel), Manchester in 1852, and Edinburgh in 1853.[114]

BRITISH FRIENDS ENTER POLITICS

An Act of Parliament of 1673 'for preventing *Dangers which may happen from Popish Recusants*' had required MPs and other holders of public office to take an Oath of Allegiance and Supremacy, and to receive holy communion according to the usage of the Church of England. John Archdale, a Quaker and a former Governor of North Carolina, had been elected to the House of Commons for Chipping Wycombe in Buckinghamshire in 1698, but as he refused on grounds of conscience to take the oath, he was deprived of his seat. In 1828, the 1673 Act and two subsequent Acts were repealed, and holders of public office were thereafter simply required to declare 'under the true Faith of a Christian,' that they would not use their office to injure, weaken, or disturb

Non-governmental peace congress in Exeter Hall, London, July 1851.

the Church of England. In 1832, Joseph Pease was elected for Durham, the first Quaker to take his seat at Westminster.

Since 1832, there has always been at least one member of the Society of Friends in the House of Commons, except for 1841–43 and 1970–71. The most eminent Quaker MP in the nineteenth century was undoubtedly John Bright. He was elected for Durham in 1843, represented Manchester from 1847 to 1857, and Birmingham from 1857 until his death in 1889. He served somewhat reluctantly in Gladstone's first Ministry as President of the Board of Trade (1868–70) and in Gladstone's second Ministry as Chancellor of the Duchy of Lancaster (1873).

In 1859, Lord Palmerston 'heard from several persons that Mr Bright would be highly flattered by being made a Privy Councillor'. Such an honour, thought Palmerston, might 'turn his thoughts and feelings into better channels . . .' But Queen Victoria firmly refused. Bright had rendered no services to the state, and a very erroneous impression would be produced if the honour were looked upon as a reward for his systematic attacks upon Britain's national institutions. Moreover, the Queen doubted whether to honour Bright would wean him from his policies, which would only gain additional weight if he were to become one of the Queen's Privy Councillors.[115] Bright automatically became a Privy Councillor when he accepted Ministerial office.

Bright was a man of great humanity and an outstanding orator, but by the standards of nineteenth century Quakerism, he could be pugnacious and, in later years, took increasing pleasure in consorting with notables. He was a staunch advocate of institutionalized methods for the peaceful settlement of disputes and of lower levels of armaments, and he opposed every war or military action in which Britain engaged during his public life. He was not a pacifist on principle, however: this issue was to him an 'abstract question', as he often called it. In a letter to the Rev. Thomas Rippon in 1882, Bright wrote:

> I have not opposed war on the ground that all war is unlawful or immoral. I will not discuss the abstract question. I shall be content when we reach the point at which all Christian men will condemn war when it is unnecessary, unjust, and leading to no useful or good result.[116]

The first Quaker peer was, I believe, Joseph Albert Pease, who took the title Lord Gainford. Pease served in Asquith's Government as Chancellor of the Duchy of Lancaster (1910–11), President of the Board of Education (1911–15), and Postmaster General (1916). He stayed in the Government after the outbreak of the first world war.

> A birthright Quaker and President of the Peace Society, a man who had always worked for peace, he faced the facts [in 1914] truly and clearly, deciding that it was the duty of the Cabinet to hold together and face the possibility of war and its evils.[117]

Pease remained a Friend, but in May 1915 he resigned the presidency of the Peace Society and was succeeded by Sir John Pease Fry, also a Friend. Pease was a founder member of the unofficial Friends League of Nations Committee, which made representations to President Wilson in 1918. He was the first chairman of the BBC.

COOPERATION WITH NON-PACIFIST PEACE-WORKERS

Throughout the nineteenth century, Friends increasingly cooperated with non-pacifist peace-workers. Friends still maintained the distinctive corporate witness that they would not bear outward arms, but they now worked with others for disarmament, the creation of a union or league of nations, the codification of international law, and arbitration or other institutionalized methods for the peaceful settlement of international disputes.[118] It was then widely believed in the peace movement, and perhaps still is, that weapons cause wars, so it was natural to oppose the accumulation of arms by Britain. Disarmament sometimes meant that Britain should reduce or eliminate its arms whatever others might do, sometimes that Britain should work for international agreements by which all states would reduce arms and totally ban categories of weapons that were regarded as particularly inhumane.

Arbitration had a wider meaning than it now has in international law. Arbitration then encompassed all methods for the peaceful settlement of international disputes, including good offices, mediation, conciliation, inquiry, judicial settlement, and arbitration in its contemporary legal meaning (third party settlement on the basis of law, the award being binding on the parties in dispute).

The most enthusiastic advocate of arbitration in the United States was Benjamin F. Trueblood, a Friend and secretary of the American Peace Society.[119] In Britain, the cause was advocated by Francis W. Fox, an ardent Quaker worker for peace and a variety of other humanitarian causes. Fox and the Baroness Bertha von Suttner were the only non-officials who were invited to attend the opening session of the inter-governmental peace conference at the Hague in 1899. In 1914, Fox drafted a proposal for a European organization for peace, with a substantial reduction of armaments and international police for enforcing peace. Another passionate proponent of third party settlement of disputes was William Randal Cremer who, though not a Friend, cooperated with Friends in peace activities. Cremer left school at the age of 12 and was first employed in a shipyard. He was active in the trade union movement, founding (with George Odger) the International Working Men's Association in 1865 and (with Fréderic Passey) the Inter-Parliamentary Union in 1890. He was for many years secretary of the International Arbitration League and was Member of Parliament for Haggerston (Shoreditch) from 1885–95 and 1900–08. Cremer and Passey were both awarded the Nobel Peace Prize.[120]

Howard Evans, a close collaborator of Cremer, described him as 'the most pugnacious of all pacifists' and a difficult man to work with, but Andrew Carnegie knew of 'no finer, more heroic life than that of Cremer.' Carnegie facilitated deputations organized by Cremer to visit Washington in 1887 and 1893 to present memorials to President Grover Cleveland in favour of an arbitration treaty between Britain and the United States. Cremer was offered a knighthood but refused as he was unwilling to wear court dress or carry a sword. King Edward VII waived the rules, so he became Sir Randal.

Andrew Carnegie's interest in international arbitration had been fostered by an American Friend, Albert Smiley, whose family owned a hotel on the beautiful shore of Lake Mohonk, near the Catskill Mountains. Beginning in 1895, Smiley organized annual conferences on international arbitration. Among the British Friends who participated in these conferences were J. Rendel Harris, the eminent Biblical scholar, and Joseph Allen Baker, a Member of Parliament and founder of the World Alliance for Promoting International Friendship through the Churches. It was as a result of the Mohonk conferences that the American Society of International Law was founded in 1906 and that Edwin Ginn established the World Peace Foundation in 1910 to promote inexpensive editions of peace classics. When Carnegie established his Endowment for International Peace in 1910, he appointed Smiley one of the founding trustees. Carnegie also provided $1.5 million for the peace palace in the Hague which is now the seat of the International Court of Justice, whose grounds were designed by George Norman Dixon, a British Friend.[121]

Andrew Carnegie and Albert Smiley.

Carnegie was confident that war could be abolished by arbitration treaties, just as duelling and slavery had been abolished in the English-speaking world by determined campaigners. In 1886, Carnegie expressed to Cremer his belief that war between civilized nations would be finally abolished in their lifetimes. Being a man of prudence, he instructed the trustees of his Endowment for Peace, using his customary simplified spelling, to abolish war and then identify the next most degrading evil or evils, 'and so on from century to century without end, my Trustees of each age shall determine how they can best aid man in his upward march to higher and higher stages of development unceasingly, for now we know that man was created . . . with the desire and the power for improvement to which, perchance, there may be no limit short of perfection even here in this life upon erth.'[122] It is now 74 years since Carnegie's death, and war is as frequent and degrading as it was in his lifetime.

The campaigners for international arbitration, in which Friends on both sides of the Atlantic played a notable part, were gratified when the inter-governmental Peace Conferences were held in the Hague in 1899 and 1907. The Baroness von Suttner, the Austrian peace-worker who persuaded Alfred Nobel to endow the Peace Prize and was herself its recipient in 1905, wrote in her diary on the day of the opening of the 1899 Conference:

> This is an epoch-making date in the history of the world . . . It is the first time, since history began to be written, that the representatives of the governments come together to find a means for 'securing a permanent, genuine peace' for the world.

But she was soon disillusioned and complaining that the delegates were merely concerned to make war more humane not to abolish it, and this has nothing to do with the organization of peace, 'nothing at all—quite the contrary!'[123]

The 1899 conference adopted resolutions on disarmament and treaties on the pacific settlement of disputes. The decisions on disarmament were in platitudinous terms and had little effect on the policies of governments. The conference simply resolved that a limitation of military expenses, which weighed heavily upon the world, was greatly to be desired. At the 1907 conference, Sir Edward Fry (a Friend and leader of the British delegation) successfully moved that the 1899 decision be re-affirmed.[124]

A strong speech in favour of compulsory arbitration was made at the 1907 conference by a Swedish delegate, Hjalmer Hammarskjold, whose son Dag was to become Secretary-General of the United Nations in 1953. The leading British advocate of international arbitration at the 1907 conference was Sir Edward Fry, whom James Scott Brown described as 'the Nestor of the Conference'.* Fry had been reluctant to head the delegation because of his ignorance of international law, diplomatic protocol, and the French language, but he finally yielded under pressure from Sir Henry Campbell-Bannerman and Sir Edward Grey. Fry celebrated his eightieth birthday during the course of the conference. After much debate, the conference amended and improved the 1899 text on international arbitration.[125]

Two of the standard books on the Hague Conferences were the result of Quaker initiatives. One was written by William I. Hull, who was professor of Quaker history at Swarthmore College from 1929 until his death ten years later and whose wife Hannah was vice-chairman of the board of the American Friends Service Committee from 1928 to 1947. The other was written by James Scott Brown as a result of a financial contribution by Eugene Levering of Baltimore, announced at the Lake Mohonk conference in 1907. Levering was of Quaker stock but became a Baptist: he stood for the US presidency in 1920 for the Prohibition Party.[126]

Nowadays we tend to take the Hague Conferences for granted, but Fry complained that the 1907 Conference did not have a good press in England and excited little public interest 'beyond avowedly pacific circles.' There were many conflicts of view and interest to be reconciled and many difficulties to be overcome. One of the delegates to the first conference told William Hull how he dealt with major differences of view.

In our delegation, when we foresaw some cloud on the horizon, we invited to dinner those whom we thought most likely to be opposed to what we considered the best solution of the problem, and, in friendly talks around the table, difficulties were smoothed away which would have been insurmountable if their disposition had been left to a committee or a commission.

But the Baroness von Suttner noted that the world was indifferent or unfriendly to the 1899 Conference, and Sir Edward Fry, with true

*Nestor was the pious and prudent mythical king of Pylos in Greece.

Quaker candour, wrote that many of the delegates to the 1907 Conference 'were more anxious to put their existence and their greatness in evidence before the world than influenced by any motives of wide philanthropy.'[127]

More and more organizations for international cooperation were now being founded: regional agencies like the Danube Commission (1856) and the Pan American Union (1889–90); what we would now call specialized agencies like the International Telegraph Union (1865) and the Universal Postal Union (1875); and international non-governmental organizations like the body that became the International Committee of the Red Cross (1863) and the World Alliance for Promoting International Friendship through the Churches (1914).

Sadly, this was to no avail in 1914. Most of the trade unionists, parliamentarians, and all those others who had so tirelessly advocated international cooperation and the peaceful settlement of disputes quickly identified themselves with the belligerent policies of their own governments. Only a minority of Church leaders remained faithful in war to the principles they had proclaimed so ardently in time of peace.

One ecumenical body was created just as the first world war broke out. The World Alliance for Promoting International Friendship through the Churches, one of the forerunners of the World Council of Churches, was the brain-child of Joseph Allen Baker, two of whose sons, Philip and Allan, were among the founders of the Friends Ambulance Unit in 1914. Allen Baker had migrated from Canada to Britain in 1876. He was active in British political and social affairs, and was MP for East Finsbury from 1905 until his death in 1918. In 1909, Benjamin Trueblood asked that Baker be invited to one of the Lake Mohonk conferences, and Baker was a regular participant thereafter. In 1911, he arranged for German participation at Mohonk, including the young Pastor Friedrich Siegmund-Schultze, and a session was held on ecumenical cooperation. Two years later, Baker approached Andrew Carnegie about the need for funds to launch a movement for ecumenical cooperation, and in 1914, after some hesitation, Carnegie provided $2 million through the Church Peace Union.* Baker initially envisaged a founding conference sponsored by British, American, and German church leaders, but he later merged his project with a separate Swiss initiative. In the end, 153 delegates from 12 countries accepted an invi-

---

*Later called the Council on Religion and International Affairs, and later still the Carnegie Council on Ethics and International Affairs.

tation to a meeting at Lake Constance (Bodensee) beginning on 1 August 1914. The circumstances were hardly propitious, and only 80 delegates completed the journey. When they held their first meeting, with Baker in the chair, the delegates were unaware that the first world war had broken out, but they were able to establish a body that in 1915 became known as the World Alliance for Promoting International Friendship Through the Churches.[128]

The World Alliance worked mainly through national councils, though international meetings were held in Czechoslovakia (1928), Britain (1931), Switzerland (1935), and Norway (1938). It was a fellowship of Christians avowedly holding divergent views. Its activities included work for war victims, the protection of minorities, advocacy of disarmament and third party settlement of disputes, the codification of international law, and the right of conscientious objectors to military service to be allowed to undertake civilian alternatives. It took the stand that 'war considered as an institution for the settlement of international disputes is incompatible with the mind and method of Christ' and that all Christian communions should declare 'in unmistakable terms' that they would not countenance nor assist any future war regarding which their government had refused international arbitration. In 1936, the World Alliance sponsored an essay contest on the theme 'The Christian Basis of Peace'. Entries were received from 38 countries: mine was awarded a bronze medal. The World Alliance was dissolved on 30 June 1948, and the World Council of Churches came into existence in Amsterdam on 23 August that year.

I am grateful to the pioneers of ecumenism. In spite of the difficulty for Friends of participation in ecumenical bodies, I have learned a great deal from Christians of other traditions. Ecumenical cooperation was a challenge to Friends of my generation: perhaps inter-Faith cooperation will be a challenge for the next generation.

QUAKER INTERNATIONAL CENTRES*

The idea of Quaker bases in key European cities originated with Carl Heath, Secretary of the National Peace Council, which had been founded in 1904 to coordinate peace efforts on a national basis. Heath was one of the speakers at a well-attended Quaker conference held in Skipton in 1917, his subject being International Reconstruction.[129] The

*These bases were variously known as Embassies, Outposts, or Settlements: increasingly from 1921, they were usually called Centres.

gist of his address was privately printed as a small pamphlet, *Quaker Embassies*.[130] Heath had joined Friends the previous June and manifested all the enthusiasm of a new convert. He believed that the first world war had demonstrated 'some deep failure in the peace movement that it should . . . break to pieces when the trumpets of war sounded . . . '

When this present storm of war is passed, we who are Quakers have a plain duty laid upon us, and that is to carry the Quaker message of the direct inner light of the Christ . . . to every great city in Europe and to every people. It is a great and a far-reaching task and one that, if carried out, will need all the faith, all the courage and all the humility the Society is capable of . . .

If we have got a word of life for the modern world it is not enough to send missions to India and China. They are needed, they do great and incalculable work for a new world, and each Quaker Mission House is a true Quaker Embassy. But we need now, after this vast disaster in Europe, true Quaker Embassies in all the great centres of the Continent for combined mission, service, study and international association.

How can it be done?

There is needed in the first place a man or a woman, or both, with experience of life, and a deep concern to carry the message to each separate country. They will be *ambassadors* for the Society.

Their homes in Paris or Petrograd, Berlin or Vienna, Rome or The Hague, Berne or Brussels, for the one or two years they can give, will be the *embassies*, and here will centre all manner of activity in close and constant touch with London. We shall certainly need a joint organizing committee, a *Foreign Office*, for this work. For the aim of an embassy will be, not merely to go to the 'foreigner', but to bring the foreigner to us. We have a message, but so have they, and the true relation of nations as members of the family of God, can only be reached when we each understand with profound and affectionate sympathy the wonderful message which each nation, and each national group, has to bring to the service of a common humanity.

The matter came before Yearly Meeting in 1918, and the minute included the following:

. . . we have been urged to take a broad view of the problems of European life, and to consider how Quaker Outposts may increasingly become centres of fellowship and inspiration to those holding or seeking the truth.[131]

In June 1918, Meeting for Sufferings asked that a conference be convened of 'Friends who are working at various aspects of this large question with a view to bringing together all the knowledge and information which has been accumulated.' The conference was duly held at Devonshire House the following month. It was agreed that a new Quaker agency should be created, the Council for International Service. Its object would be the linking up and coordinating of all existing work abroad and advancing the delivery of the Quaker message as way may open. The conference hoped that settlements would be established 'for the study of prevailing conditions, and from which our Message may be given, not only by the lips but by the lives of those who have responded to the call to this service.' There had been some criticism of the idea that these outposts should be called Quaker Embassies, but Carl Heath said he was 'prepared to defend the term as being not only correct but desirable', and the conference agreed that the term Quaker Embassies was the right one. Irish and American Friends were invited to cooperate with the new agency, which held its first meeting in February 1919.[132] Carl Heath became chairman of the new Council for International Service, and in 1920 its secretary. In 1927, the Council merged with the Friends Foreign Mission Association (which had been formed in 1868 but had not been officially recognized by London Yearly Meeting until 1917) to form the Friends Service Council, one of the founding bodies of Quaker Peace and Service.

Seven international centres arose directly from war-time and post-war relief: three in Germany (Berlin, Frankfurt, and Nürnberg), together with Vienna, Paris, Warsaw, and Moscow. A new centre was established in Geneva in 1922, and the report of the Council for International Service in 1924 refers also to centres in Essen and Elberfeld.[133] There was a centre in Salonika in the 1920s, and a short-term centre in the Saar for three months in 1935.[134] In most cases, there was close coordination between the London committees, the American Friends Service Committee, and local Friends.

There was a renewed spurt of enthusiasm in the critical years 1939–41. Dutch Friends opened a centre in 1939, Scandinavian Friends joined in establishing a centre in Copenhagen in 1940, and a centre was opened in London in 1941. One international centre was opened outside Europe in 1939, that in Shanghai, sponsored by the Friends Service Council. This was not primarily related to Chinese conditions but to care for European refugees from Nazi oppression.[135]

The centres in Europe were used to promote and coordinate peace work, for reconciling activities in areas of inter-communal or international tension, to draw the attention of leaders to the needs of minorities, to report to home committees on local conditions, including violations of human rights and threats to peace,[136] and (especially in the early years) for the circulation of Quaker literature.

The activities varied from centre to centre, and at different periods. During the 1920s, the emphasis in Berlin and Vienna was on reconciliation between former enemies. Conferences were run by the Berlin centre on Germany's relations with France and Poland, and efforts were made to publicize Germany's economic difficulties under the reparations clauses of the Versailles Treaty. With the rise of totalitarianism in the 1930s, attention was also directed to the human rights of the victims of Nazi oppression. Corder Catchpool had a special concern for German minorities outside the Reich, and this led him to pay three visits to Lithuania to investigate the condition of German prisoners from the Memel area (1935, 1936 and 1938), and he was later to concern himself with the welfare of Sudeten Germans in Czechoslovakia.[137]

The centres in Essen and Elberfeld were evidently short-lived, and those in Frankfurt and Nürnberg were handed over to local Friends in 1934 and 1935 respectively.[138]

The Vienna Centre acted as a base for coordinating the activities of Austrian peace organizations. After 1934, it functioned as a centre for the relief of socialist prisoners after the unsuccessful revolt against Dollfuss; and after the *anschluss* in 1938, help was given to political dissidents and persons of Jewish ancestry.[139]

The Paris Centre was used for peace activities, work among students, penal reform, the rights of conscientious objectors to military service, the care of refugees, and as the headquarters of *L'Entr'Aide Européenne*.[140]

The Centre in Moscow was never a very solid enterprise. One American nurse, Anna Haines, did a variety of jobs under the Moscow Health Department until 1926, and the British worker, Dorice White, supported herself by giving English lessons until the lease of the Quaker premises was terminated by the Soviet authorities in 1931.[141]

The main focus of the Warsaw Centre was on relations between Poland and Germany. The Warsaw and Berlin Centres cooperated in organizing three conferences on German-Polish relations (1925–27), and in arranging for a party of young Germans to visit Warsaw (1926). The Warsaw Centre also helped in the establishment of a council of Polish pacifist organizations.[142]

The Geneva Centre differed from the others in that it had not originated in war-time relief. It served as a liaison office with the League of Nations and other international agencies. Bertram and Irene Pickard, who arrived in 1926, soon became familiar figures in the diplomatic community and among organizations concerned with peace and disarmament. Bertram Pickard was an able writer and reported regularly to various periodicals on League of Nations matters. He was later to be appointed to the office in the United Nations Secretariat for keeping contact with non-governmental organizations.[143]

Heath's vision led to some semantic confusion. A Quaker Embassy or International Centre was to be a base of operations for a Quaker ambassador or ambassadors from Britain, whereas a Quaker base with similar activities but run by indigenous Quakers was not termed an International Centre. Thus Warsaw was regarded as an International Centre, but not Prague. In 1921, John William Hoyland, warden of a centre in Britain for training overseas workers, was moved to say, 'When we say we have a . . . centre in Warsaw, for example, it may convey the idea that we have a number of maintained workers there . . . I don't think we have anyone even on half pay there, have we?'[144]

The truth was that the reality of the international centres between the wars never quite matched Carl Heath's vision. At first, workers who had engaged in war and post-war relief were available for staffing the centres, but gradually most of these people returned to normal family life and employment. Some of the centres were eventually turned over to the management of local Friends, continuing as bases for local Quaker activities but hardly qualifying as Quaker Embassies. The Warsaw and Moscow centres were closed by the authorities in 1929 and 1931 respectively. Thus the eleven international centres of the 1920s had by 1938 dwindled to four: Berlin, Vienna, Paris and Geneva.

Heath's original idea was that British Friends had 'a word of life for the modern world', to be taken to the main European capitals by Quaker ambassadors who would be 'in close and constant touch with London.' What he seems not to have envisaged, at any rate initially, was that war-time and post-war relief, supplemented by the network of international centres, would lead to the development of small but enthusiastic Quaker groups on the continent. Increasingly, these Friends wanted to run their own affairs, and in some places, the presence of foreign Quaker 'ambassadors' could be a source of embarrassment—in the Soviet Union and Poland in the 1920s, in Germany and Austria in the 1930s. Local Friends in the latter two countries undertook humanitarian work for the victims of Nazism, but unobtrusively. Foreign Friends engaging in similar work were inevitably more visible. Corder Catchpool was arrested in Berlin in 1933 and in Prague in 1938, and Elizabeth Fox Howard was detained by the Gestapo in 1935. Moreover, the 1935 statement of Meeting for Sufferings on Nazi excesses seemed to some German Friends to be verging from the humanitarian realm into the political, at a time when German Friends were stressing that they were simply a *religious* society.

Corder Catchpool in Berlin took the line that he would help victims of oppression without discrimination. He was as willing to go to the aid of a victimized Nazi as of a victimized Jew or Gypsy. It was in this spirit that he interceded for German prisoners in Lithuania, some of whom were undoubtedly Nazi thugs, and sought to give aid and comfort to the Sudeten Germans in Czechoslovakia, while realizing that some of them engaged in provocative and bellicose activities. Corder Catchpool always saw the best in people: after meeting Konrad Henlein, the Sudeten Nazi leader, he wrote: 'he gave the impression of a straightforward, moderate and able man.'[145]

Geneva was in some ways the most successful international centre, certainly the most permanent, for it still exists. It is located in a city that remains stubbornly Swiss, but with an increasing international population for staffing inter-governmental and non-governmental agencies. Here, as in other cities, there was sometimes tension between the international centre, with its foreign Quaker supporters, and the small group of dispersed local Quakers.

FRIENDS AND THE PEACE MOVEMENTS BETWEEN THE WARS
Carl Heath would have been the first to agree that work for peace begins at home. Between the two world wars, this Quaker activity was

on much the same lines as during the previous hundred years: the dissemination of literature, the organization of meetings, participation in non-governmental peace conferences. There was little in the way of demonstrative action on the lines of the Jarrow Hunger Marches of the 1930s or the Aldermaston Marches after the second world war. The one peace innovation between the wars was the Peace Ballot of 1934–35, organized by the League of Nations Union, in which more than eleven million people took part. The result of the ballot was as follows:

Voting yes

1. Should Great Britain remain a member of the League of Nations? — 96%
2. Are you in favour of an all-round reduction in armaments by international agreement? — 91%
3. Are you in favour of an all-round abolition of national military and naval aircraft by international agreement? — 82%
4. Should the manufacture and sale of armaments for private profit be prohibited by international agreement? — 90%
5. Do you consider that, if a nation insists on attacking another, the other nations should combine to compel it to stop by
   (a) Economic and non-military measures? — 87%
   (b) If necessary, military measures? — 59%

I voted yes to all questions except 5(b).

The substance of peace propaganda between the wars was the wickedness, waste, and futility of war as an instrument of national policy, support for the League of Nations, advocacy of disarmament, and stress on the right of conscientious objection to military service.

The majority of British Friends were happy to cooperate with other peace-workers. The following dozen were some of the organizations for peace in which Friends were prominently engaged between the wars.

National Peace Council
Union of Democratic Control
Fellowship of Reconciliation
Women's International League for Peace and Freedom

League of Nations Union
International Voluntary Service for Peace
No More War Movement
War Resisters' International
Peace Pledge Union
Embassies of Reconciliation
No-Conscription League
Federal Union

In addition, a number of Friends like Philip Noel-Baker and Inazo Nitobe were employed in the League of Nations Secretariat.

PEACE WORK IN WAR-TIME
There are limits to what peace-workers can do when their country is at war. The majority of young Quaker men and women were performing alternative service or were in prison during the second world war, and those who were free to undertake peace work gave much time to the rights of conscientious objectors to military service. To protest against particular acts of war that were inhumane or contrary to international law might have seemed to imply that war can be a civilized process if the belligerents only keep to the rules. To advocate negotiations with the enemy can easily be represented as sympathy for the enemy's war aims. These were predicaments faced by Friends on both sides during the second world war. Roger Wilson, in his Pendle Hill lectures in 1943, had this to say.

> Some pacifists . . . who plead in political terms for an immediate armistice or for negotiations now with Hitler . . . appear to assume that a reliance on man's capacity for goodness naturally produces good results. There is no evidence for this assumption . . . [W]e Christian pacifists, as such have nothing to say on the immediate political problems in which the world has to find a day-by-day answer.

Six years later, in his Swarthmore Lecture, Wilson repeated the last sentence, but changed 'Christian pacifists . . . have nothing to say' to 'I do not believe that we Christian pacifists have much to say'.[146]

The one peace activity in which British Friends were able to engage during the war was in planning a new international organization to replace the discredited League of Nations.

EAST–WEST RELATIONS

It may seem strange to some Friends in 1993 to learn how much Quaker energy was directed to the easing of Cold War tensions in the first two decades after the second world war. Scholars are not agreed on the date on which the Cold War broke out. I first became aware that all was not well with inter-Allied relations at the time of the Yalta conference in February 1945, but other writers date the onset of the Cold War to the early months of 1946, with difficulties at the United Nations over Iran, Greece, Indonesia, and nuclear issues. It was natural that Friends should ask themselves whether they were called to undertake a reconciling role over East–West difficulties, and in 1946, the Friends Peace Committee formed a Russia Group chaired by Geoffrey Wilson, who had served in the Moscow embassy with Sir Stafford Cripps during the second world war.[147] In 1950, the work in this field was formally upgraded and extended geographically by Meeting for Sufferings, which established the East–West Relations Group to undertake studies for the relief of East-West tensions.[148]

One of the first issues we had to face was the relationship of the new Group to the Partizans of Peace (later called the World Peace Council) and its British affiliate, the British Peace Committee. The Partizans of Peace had originated with a conference of intellectuals held in Wrocław (formerly Breslau) in Poland in 1948 and the International Liaison Committee of Intellectuals for Peace which had met in Paris in 1949. At the latter conference, it was decided to convene a mammoth World Peace Congress in Stockholm in 1950, and this Congress adopted a resolution, known as the Stockholm Peace Appeal, in the following terms.

We demand the unconditional prohibition of the atomic weapon as an instrument of aggression and mass extermination of people, and the establishment of strict international control over the fulfilment of this decision.

We will regard as a war criminal that government which first uses the atomic weapon against any country.

We call upon all people of goodwill all over the world to sign this call.

It was decided at Stockholm to hold another big peace congress in Sheffield the following November, but as the British Government decided to deny entry-permits to known Communists and fellow-travellers, the Congress was transferred to Warsaw, where the sponsoring body was re-named the World Peace Council (WPC). By 1951, the WPC had become even more closely identified with Soviet foreign policy, and it was widely thought that the Soviet Union may have intended to build it up as an alternative to the UN.[149]

Friends had not been officially represented at any of these WPC events, though some Friends participated in personal capacities or as representatives of non-Quaker organizations. Members of the East–West Relations Group disliked the large scale of the WPC conferences and we were reluctant to participate unless we could share in the drafting of the agenda, the choice of participants and speakers, and the preparation of draft resolutions. This last was a point of special difficulty, because while we often agreed with what was said in the WPC resolutions, we wished to include other points in order to make the resolutions more balanced. Thus in October 1950, Friends had agreed with the WPC that forces of the Unified Command in Korea ought not to have crossed the 38th parallel into North Korea, but we also took the line that North Korea should not have invaded South Korea the previous June.

When the East-West Relations Group was established in 1950, we at once made contact with the Soviet and several of the East European embassies in London, and shortly thereafter we received overtures from the British Peace Committee. We explained why we were unable to send official Quaker delegations to large WPC conferences, but suggested two alternatives: a private meeting between the East-West Relations Group and a similar number from the WPC, and a small Quaker mission to the Soviet Union. We discussed the latter idea with Soviet diplomats in London early in 1951.

The private meeting we had suggested took place at Charney Manor in April 1951 and was, I believe, a useful occasion. During a private conversation between sessions, we raised the question of a British Quaker delegation to the Soviet Union with the Soviet participant (Aleksander Evokimovic Korneichuk, a writer, presiding officer of the Ukrainian Soviet, and a member of the Central Committee of the Soviet Communist Party). Shortly thereafter, the Soviet Peace Committee invited British Friends to send up to eight members to the Soviet Union during the course of the summer. The visit took place between 15 and 27 July. Only two requests were made to the hosts in advance: that the delegation not be offered alcoholic beverages, and that they be allowed some time to themselves each day.[150]

The mission had a threefold purpose: to take a message of goodwill to the Soviet people from British Quakers, to find out something of the position of religion in the Soviet Union, and 'to discuss with influential people of all kinds the methods that must be used to achieve peace and understanding.' The hosts of the delegation in Moscow, Leningrad (as it then was), and Kiev were the local sections of the Soviet Peace Committee. Their representatives 'were anxious to concentrate on points of agreement, but Friends thought it more profitable . . . to discuss points of difference in order to see if any understanding or reconciliation of opposing views were possible.' Wherever they went, the Quaker delegates were asked why Friends did not support the Stockholm Peace Appeal or send delegations to the gigantic conferences of the World Peace Council. The Quaker delegation did not question the sincerity of the many supporters of the World Peace Council in the Soviet Union and other countries, but they claimed that the documents and speeches of the WPC were often 'belligerent, and not reconciling . . . not couched in the language of peace or of understanding.' The Quaker group could not believe that peace could be built on a campaign of hatred and vilification. They did not doubt that the Soviet people wished for peace at least as eagerly as the peoples elsewhere, but they concluded that the WPC was a movement designed 'to improve the bargaining power of the Soviet Union rather than to promote real reconciliation.'[151]

On the penultimate day of the visit, the Quaker group had a meeting with Yaacov Malik, a senior official at the Soviet Foreign Office, to discuss a paper which had been submitted to him in writing several days previously. This contained seven suggestions for reciprocal action by the Soviet Union and the West: restraint in hostile propaganda against the other side, opening-up of contacts between professional groups, pledges of non-interference in the domestic affairs of other countries, radical and internationally-controlled disarmament, a UN plan for economic aid to raise living standards throughout the world, admission to the UN of all applicant states, and great-power consultations at the summit to agree on principles to implement these proposals.[152]

Malik's oral reply was that the Soviet Union already favoured and was implementing all seven suggestions. The Soviet Union 'does not conduct hostile propaganda against other countries'; 'there is no ban on the exchange of delegations . . . nor is there any ban on correspondence'; 'The Soviet Union strictly carries out the provision of the [UN] Charter as to non-interference'; 'the Soviet Union has on many occasions introduced its proposal for . . . the reduction of arms and the immediate prohibition of atomic weapons'; 'the Soviet Union [has] proposed the provision of technical assistance to economically backward countries'; 'the Soviet Union stands for the admission of all these States [some but *not all* of the applicants] to the United Nations'; 'The Soviet Union has on many occasions taken steps designed to arrive at an agreement on all important questions.'[153]

Anyone reading the account of the interview more than four decades after the event will be struck by the bland and evasive nature of Malik's comments, but would not a Soviet delegation meeting a British minister at the height of the Cold War have had a similar experience?

The visit, both within Quaker circles and among much of the wider public, was judged to have been a success. Two of the purposes had been achieved: to convey goodwill and to discuss methods of achieving peace and understanding. The third purpose, to find out about religion in the Soviet Union, had been achieved in part: contact had been made with Christian leaders, but not with adherents of other Faiths. *The Manchester Guardian* (as it then was) had been sufficiently impressed by the report of the visit to suggest the following year that Quakers should investigate Communist allegations that the United States had resorted to germ warfare in Korea.[154]

A concern now arose to send a mission to China. This proved impossible while the fighting was taking place in Korea, but following contacts between Friends and Chinese delegates to the Geneva Conference on Korea and Indo-China in 1954,[155] an invitation was received from the Chinese Peace Committee. The visit took place in 1955, three of the six members of the Quaker team having previously worked in China. As had been the case of the mission to the Soviet Union, Friends asked in advance that alcoholic drinks not be served.[156]

The Quaker visitors encountered friendliness everywhere, but the Chinese showed little curiosity about life in Britain. There was much discussion about ways of achieving peace, but the Chinese did not refer to the Stockholm Peace Appeal, nor did they reproach Friends for not taking part in the activities of the World Peace Council. As in the Soviet Union, Friends made contact with Chinese Christians when possible.

The mission did not take with them a set of written suggestions for achieving peace, as had the delegation to the Soviet Union: instead, they had a statement in English and Chinese about Quaker beliefs and practices.

At the end of the visit, the team had an interview with Zhou Enlai (Chou En-lai), at that time Prime Minister and Foreign Minister, who had had contact with members of the Friends Ambulance Unit in Chongquing (Chungking) and Yenan. It seems, from the published report, to have been a relaxed occasion, and Zhou exhibited his customary urbanity. Zhou said that China could wait a hundred years for US recognition—though in fact China took its seat at the United Nations sixteen years later, and full diplomatic relations between the United States and China were established in 1979. He indicated that American Friends would be welcome in China whenever they wished to pay a visit, and an AFSC delegation did indeed visit China in 1972. Zhou said he favoured more cultural contacts with other countries and an end to abusive propaganda.

The third delegation to a Communist country in which British Friends participated was to Poland in 1957. The previous year, Włady-sław Gomułka, who had been 'purged' in 1949 and imprisoned in 1951 for ideological deviations, was released. He was elected leader of the United Workers (Communist) Party in October. He denounced the terrorism of the Stalinist period and freed Cardinal Stefan Wyszynski from detention. This process of relative liberalization was widely known as the Polish October.

There were eight members of the Quaker delegation, three from Britain, two from the continent of Europe, and three from the United States. We were not the guests of the Peace Committee, as had been the case with the missions to the Soviet Union and China, but of the semi-detatched Polish Institute of International Affairs. By the time we reached Poland, all the talk there was of the dictum of Mao Zedong (Mao Tse-tung) six months previously, that a hundred flowers should be allowed to bloom and a hundred schools of thought allowed to contend. We were, indeed, struck by the 'remarkable degree of freedom of thought and discussion.'[157]

The purposes of the visit were much the same as those of the two previous delegations to Communist countries, but we also stressed our wish to renew contacts established by Quaker relief workers after the two world wars. Poland seemed to us to be 'a Communist state with a difference.' The Polish October had represented 'a peaceful revolution', and we were impressed with the relatively flexible and pragmatic way in which Communist theories were being applied. The strong system of centralized control before 1956 had caused 'social dislocation and economic disequilibrium', and we heard a good deal about 'problems of social demoralization.'

We held a meeting for worship with the small group of Polish Friends and sympathizers, and we made contact with many of the Churches and with the Jewish community. We were told by Jewish leaders that there was some anti-Semitism at that time but that this was not an especially acute problem.

We met a number of political leaders, and had a constructive discussion on foreign affairs with Josef Winiewicz, the Deputy Foreign Minister, who had been a frequent visitor to Quaker House in New York. Because of Poland's geopolitical situation, he said, Poland had to have close relations with the Soviet Union, but Poland could take limited international initiatives—as, indeed, happened shortly after our visit when Foreign Minister Adam Rapacki proposed in the UN General Assembly that Poland, Czechoslovakia, and the two parts of Germany should constitute a zone free of nuclear weapons.

Our three main impressions were of the very great friendship shown to us by all sections of the community, the great enthusiasm for the new trends following the Polish October, and that 'essential human problems are the same in all parts of the world.'

At a less official Quaker level, young Friends from Britain and the United States had also been initiating or participating in meetings and exchanges with East Europeans: conferences, seminars, work camps, work and study projects, and the like. They did not find it easy participating in big Communist-led events. There were cases of biased chairing, in which the floor was given to Communist speakers to introduce resolutions or reply to attacks, while the same right was denied to Westerners. There was often no real debate.

> After the meeting had been thrown open, prospective speakers would send up their names on pieces of paper . . . The speaker would then usually read a prepared statement, often of great length . . . [I]t was rare for a speaker to have modified his position as a result of what he had learnt from the conference and even rarer for him to take up any point made by the previous speaker. An assort-

ment of rigid, irreconcilable positions were stockpiled, but it is doubtful whether anyone had increased his understanding of what moved other people to say what they did, or had even seriously listened.[158]

The visit to Poland had been jointly sponsored by the Friends Service Council and the American Friends Service Committee. Other goodwill missions to Communist countries organized by the AFSC alone included Yugoslavia (1950), the Soviet Union (1955), the German Democratic Republic (and the Federal Republic) (1963), Cuba (1969 and 1981), China (1972), Kampuchea and Vietnam (1982), North Korea (1984), and North Korea (and South Korea) (1991).[159]

The year after the visit to Poland, a new peace movement began in Eastern Europe, the Christian Peace Conference, with its head-quarters in Prague. This was somewhat less of a mouth-piece for Soviet foreign policy than the World Peace Council had been. Richard Ullmann and six other Friends, including one from the German Democratic Republic, attended the founding Conference in Czechoslovakia in 1959.

Ullmann later made it clear that he participated in this and subsequent gatherings 'with much inner reservation'. The Quaker reconciler, he wrote, was tempted to resort to clever verbal formulations, unclear expressions, or dubious ambiguities in order to reach a vague consensus with East European Christians. The choice often seemed to be between truth and love. But Ullmann concluded that we must pay the price of this conflict, of anxiety and spiritual suffering, if we wish to be the disciples of Jesus in this service. The conflict is most poignant when it comes to the problem of appeasement, he wrote, for we are tempted to buy outward peace by sacrificing third parties. Ullmann cites an example from 1959, when East European Christians proposed that 6 August, the anniversary of the dropping of the first atomic bomb, should be designated 'a Day of Repentance'. The Westerners pointed out that such a call from Prague would be understood in the West as a denunciation of the United States, so that the appeal would be divisive and not unifying. The Westerners suggested that 'Repentance' should be changed to 'Prayer', as a sign that Christians everywhere were more concerned with present and future sin than with the sins of the past. In the end, this was agreed.[160]

By the 1960s, Friends were still doing useful work regarding East-

West Relations, but no longer of the pioneering nature of the previous fifteen years. Other groups—scientists, trade unionists, church members, peace activists—were making contact with their opposite numbers in the Soviet Union. The Great Britain-USSR Association had been founded in 1959, and in 1964, the British Council of Churches had appointed the Rev. Paul Oestreicher to handle relations with Eastern Europe.[161] In 1965, after several years of dithering, the East-West Relations Committee asked to be laid down, and its residual functions were taken over by the newly-formed Friends Peace and International Relations Committee.

The reconciler faces many poignant moments of decision. When I was in Moscow in the 1950s, I realized that in a period of nine days it was necessary to be selective in what I would do, so I decided to concentrate on three things: a certain amount of conventional sight-seeing as a courtesy to my hosts, to examine the various institutions in the Soviet capital concerned with the United Nations, and to visit every place of religious worship that I could find. My young guide was puzzled that a person of normal intelligence should be interested in anything as obscurantist as religion!

For the last evening of the visit we had tickets for the Bolshoi Ballet, but my guide asked if we could instead go to the Gorki Park of Rest and Culture for a private talk. She had already told me a good deal about her life, her family situation, and her job. She now said that she abhorred the Soviet system, and had reached a turning point. She had three choices: to join what she called the underground movement, a shadowy organization that engaged in small and apparently futile acts of industrial sabotage; to go abroad as an interpreter with a Soviet delegation, and then become a refugee; or to continue leading a double life, saying things during her working day that she knew were untrue and spending her leisure hours with friends and enjoying Russian literature, art, music, and other aesthetic pleasures. 'You are a man of honour: which option do you recommend?'

What I said in reply is not now of great importance. One of my friends later suggested that she was an *agent provocateur*, but I doubt it: we kept in touch by correspondence for many years, her letters being posted in various countries, but never in the Soviet Union. But I often think of that conversation when I come across those in the secular world who have to choose between courses of action all of which seem either futile, hazardous, or immoral.

QUAKER WORK AT THE UNITED NATIONS

The UN Charter was adopted at the founding conference at San Francisco on 26 June 1945 and entered into force the following October. At that stage, no decision had been reached about the location of the headquarters for the new organization, and the first session of the UN General Assembly convened in Westminster Central Hall in bomb-scarred London, with the Secretariat located in the nearby Church House. In 1946, it was decided to establish permanent headquarters in New York City, with a European office in the Palais des Nations in Geneva, which had been the headquarters of the League of Nations. The UN Secretariat building on Manhattan's east side was completed in stages in 1950–51, and the General Assembly building was ready in time for the annual session in the autumn in 1952.

British Friends were in general supportive of the new effort to create an international organization to promote cooperation and preserve peace. In March 1945, eight weeks before the opening of the San Francisco Conference, Meeting for Sufferings adopted a long statement welcoming the organization about to be born. Friends stressed the inter-dependent nature of the modern world, the dangers arising from competition for power, the need for trust among nations, and the value of procedures for third-party settlement of disputes. The work of the International Labour Organization and other technical agencies was commended, and a plea was made for the needs of the oppressed. 'May it be given to you to meet these needs and to set up for all men, for they are all God's people, a habitation fit to dwell in.'[162]

Friends had proposed in 1920 that meetings of the Assembly of the League of Nations should begin with 'a period of devotional silence'. This proposal was not adopted, but it was renewed for the UN, and the rules of procedure for the General Assembly provide that at the beginning of the first meeting of each session and at the end of the last meeting, 'the President shall invite the representatives to observe one minute of silence dedicated to prayer or meditation.'[163] Friends were also one of the non-governmental organizations that persuaded Secretary-General Trygve Lie that the UN building should include a Meditation Room: this is located at the north end of the main floor of the General Assembly building.[164]

UN Secretary-General Dag Hammarskjold took a personal interest in the Meditation Room and wrote a leaflet for those who might use it. Extracts from the leaflet follow.

Meditation Room at the United Nations Headquarters, New York.

We all have within us a centre of stillness surrounded by silence.

This house, dedicated to work and debate in the service of peace, should have one room dedicated to silence in the outward sense and stillness in the inner sense.

It has been the aim to create in this small room a place where the doors may be open to the infinite lands of thought and prayer.

People of many faiths will meet here, and for that reason none of the symbols to which we are accustomed in our meditation could be used.

However, there are simple things which speak to us all with the same language. We have sought for such things and we believe that we have found them . . .

There is an ancient saying that the sense of a vessel is not in its shell but in the void. So it is with this room. It is for those who come here to fill the void with what they find in their center of stillness.

The League of Nations Covenant had made no provision for relations with non-governmental organizations, but the UN Charter provided that the UN Economic and Social Council (ECOSOC) might make 'suitable arrangements for consultation' with national or international non-governmental organizations regarding matters within ECOSOC's competence (Article 71). It had been agreed by the main Quaker agencies that activities at the UN should be under the auspices of the Friends World Committee for Consultation (FWCC), but that the actual work in New York should be administered by the American Friends Service Committee (AFSC). The situation in Geneva was more complicated as there was already an international centre there, administered jointly by the AFSC and the Friends Service Council. Joint administration provided endless headaches. Two-thirds of the funding came from Philadelphia, one-third from London, so accounts had to be kept in three different currencies—and the financial years of the administering agencies did not coincide. Administrative responsibility for the Geneva centre was transferred to FSC in the 1960s.

In 1947, AFSC established a centre on East 52nd Street in Manhattan, initially staffed by Philip and Lois Jessup. Philip Jessup became Ambassador-at-Large for President Truman in 1949 and later served as a judge at the International Court of Justice in the Hague (1961–70).

The Jessups were succeeded in New York by Elmore and Beth Jackson. In 1953, AFSC purchased a brownstone house in East 48th Street, now known as Quaker House, a couple of blocks from the UN headquarters building. A main purpose of the Quaker operation at the UN, according to Clarence Pickett, was to strengthen the moral and spiritual values of UN delegates and officials.[165]

In March 1948, the FWCC was granted consultative status at the UN. This enabled Quaker representatives to attend meetings of ECOSOC and its subsidiary organs and, under prescribed conditions, to circulate written documents or make oral statements. In 1956, British Friends established a UN Consultative Committee, succeeded in 1965 by a UN and Disarmament Working Group, which in turn was succeeded in 1978 by the UN Committee of Quaker Peace and Service.

Technically, FWCC's status at the UN is confined to economic and social matters, but once Quaker representatives have access to UN buildings, there is nothing to prevent them from lobbying the delegates about other issues of Quakerly concern. When I arrived in New York in 1954, I was asked to handle three matters. The first was economic affairs, but in 1955, staff responsibilities were re-assigned and I handed over most economic matters to an American colleague. The only matter with economic implications that I dealt with thereafter was the possibility of assigning one or more Quaker-sponsored volunteers to one of the UN's aid programmes. In this latter case, we had a small success in 1957, when a British conscientious objector from the FAU International Service was accepted to work with the UN technical assistance programme in Iran.[166] The other two subjects that I was asked to deal with were disarmament and decolonization, neither of which came within the purview of ECOSOC and for neither of which did Friends have any official standing at the UN.

A major asset in both New York and Geneva has been the existence of Quaker centres (and, since 1961, William Penn House in London) where we could hold private conversations or round-table discussions with UN diplomats.

Let me give an example of the unique role of Quaker House in New York. In 1957, the UN General Assembly decided to create an Economic Commission for Africa.[167] At that stage, there were eight African Members of the UN plus South Africa. The UN Secretariat needed to consult UN Member-States in Africa about a host of technical issues, such as the location of the headquarters of the new Commission. The

William Epstein and Otto Frey, joint heads of the United Nations Disarmament Section, and Sydney Bailey, outside the UN Security Council Chamber in 1956.

apartheid issue had been before the UN General Assembly since 1952, however, and it was inconceivable that diplomats from Black Africa would meet in the same room in the UN building as a White South African diplomat. The UN Under-Secretary concerned asked whether Friends would invite him and the African delegates to a private and informal lunch at Quaker House. After discreet inquiries, we learned that all would accept an invitation from the Quakers, and a very fruitful but private meeting took place.

Another asset was the fact that many UN diplomats had had previous experience of Quakers. Perhaps I may give one example. After the Hungarian revolt of 1956, Dean Rusk (then president of the Rockefeller Foundation) visited Budapest to investigate relief needs. On his return, Rusk phoned me to say that he had been very impressed with the recently-reconstituted Hungarian Red Cross and that he was recommending to his trustees the dispatch of a major consignment of relief supplies. The Foundation was, however, precluded from supplying 'consumables', and 20,000 square metres of X-ray film were urgently needed. Could the Quakers help?

I transmitted the request to Philadelphia the same day, and within a matter of hours, a grant of $10,000 had been approved. The following day, I arranged to meet a member of the Hungarian delegation to tell him about the grant and to make sure that he understood the non-political nature of Quaker service and, in particular, the fact that we had Quaker workers at the camp for Hungarian refugees at Traiskirchen in Austria. I told him about my previous discussions with the Hungarian Foreign Minister (Imre Horvath) about our willingness to provide humanitarian relief, and of our concern for improving East-West relations by means of personal contacts. I stressed that we were caring for Hungarian refugees in Austria, whom he undoubtedly would regard as enemies of the régime.

The Hungarian official sat very impassively through all this, and I was afraid I was not articulating the Quaker position clearly enough or that his knowledge of English was not good. Suddenly he interrupted me and said, 'You need not tell me anything about Quakers, because they saved my son's life.' My Hungarian friend had taken part in the failed Communist coup in Hungary in 1919, and had then taken refuge in Austria. When the Nazi *anschluss* had taken place in 1938, he had gone underground, and the Quaker centre had arranged for his son to go to Britain, where he had been adopted by a Quaker family in Yorkshire. My Hungarian friend hoped to visit his son as soon as the UN General Assembly adjourned.[168]

Two special activities of the UN offices in New York during the 1950s should be mentioned. The first was the publication of studies relating to UN issues. One, a book on the peaceful settlement of disputes, was issued before my arrival.[169] I had a small hand in another, *The Future Development of the United Nations*,[170] though when I re-read it recently, I found it rather bland and uninspiring.

The other special activity was the arrival during the General Assembly each year of an international Quaker team.[171] The advantage of this arrangement was that, for part of the year at any rate, the Quaker presence at the UN was not exclusively Anglo-Saxon. The inclusion in the team of Friends from Mexico, Sweden, or Kenya forced the permanent Quaker staff and committee to view UN issues more broadly than would otherwise have been the case. The difficulty was that assembling and maintaining a team of, say, four Friends from around the world for six or eight weeks was immensely time-consuming and expensive. With a few exceptions, the team members had no previous experience of the UN—which entrance to use, where to sit in UN meetings, how to contact the delegates, and so on. The result was that the permanent staff spent much of the time during the General Assembly guiding the visiting Friends. Personally I thought the effort was, on balance, worthwhile, and I was sorry when the practice was dropped in the 1970s.

FRIENDS (AND OTHERS) IN THE UN SYSTEM

Another asset for the Quaker offices in New York and Geneva was to find Friends or near-Friends in the UN system. When I was at the Quaker office in New York in the 1950s, we were in touch with about thirty Friends in the UN Secretariat and among the delegates. We started a weekly meeting for worship at Quaker House for people working in and around the UN.

The Quaker offices at the UN in New York and Geneva operate under the general umbrella of the Friends World Committee for Consultation, but occasionally individual Friends undertook activities at the UN under other Quaker auspices. One American Yearly Meeting appointed its own representative at the UN, and she was constantly quarrelling with UN guards who denied her access to parts of the UN building that she was not entitled to enter. On one occasion, the sec-

Sydney D. Bailey presenting a set of his books on the United Nations to Secretary-General Waldheim.

retary of an AFSC regional office petitioned the UN Trusteeship Council in protest against US nuclear testing in the vicinity of a UN Trust Territory in the Pacific. In the Quaker UN office, we had opposed *all* nuclear testing by *all* states in *all* environments, but we had taken the line that action on this issue was a matter for the UN's disarmament bodies and not for the Trusteeship Council, the functions of which are carefully defined in the UN Charter.

One evening, I by chance discovered a staff member of another AFSC office who for several days had been 'fasting unto death' in the UN Meditation Room in protest against nuclear testing, spending his nights in a nearby church. As it happened, the AFSC UN Committee was meeting in half an hour, and I reported the circumstances to the Committee. They admired the intentions of the young man but thought that the location of his witness was misconceived. For one thing, the UN as an institution conducted no nuclear tests and had no way of achieving the object of the young man's sacrificial action. The Committee also thought that it was a misuse of the Meditation Room, which had been set up so that UN delegates, officials, and members of the public could spend time in prayer or meditation in a non-sectarian atmosphere. The Committee agreed to invite the young man to attend part of the Committee meeting and to elaborate his concern.[172]

I was asked to find out whether there were circumstances in which our young friend would terminate this fast other than the unconditional ending of nuclear testing. After many conversations, and in a weakened state of health, he agreed to call off his fast if he could explain his concern to UN Secretary-General Dag Hammarskjold. There were two difficulties about this. First, Hammarskjold was not in New York at the time but on a five-week peace mission to the Middle East. Secondly, Hammarskjold's office took the view that to meet the request would create an unfortunate precedent: if the request were conceded, the UN Meditation Room would soon be overflowing with concerned individuals fasting unto death in order to get an appointment with the UN Secretary-General! In the end, we negotiated an agreement by which the young man would explain his concern to a UN Under-Secretary. He did this with great aplomb, and the Under-Secretary listened with appropriate sensitivity.

In our work at the UN, we received much help and encouragement from non-Quaker men and women in the UN community. Most of the original members of the UN Secretariat were idealists who had experienced the horrors of the second world war and wanted to do their bit in building a better world. They were true internationalists, committed to the ideals of the United Nations. Unhappily, the number of idealists in the UN Secretariat has diminished as a quota system for staff appointments has been introduced and the proportion of short-term secondments from national governments has increased.

The delegates all act under instructions, even if the instruction is simply to follow the NATO line or vote with India.[173] Many of the delegates are prisoners of national ideology, and the task of all of them is to promote the national interest. They are not without principles, however, and the best of them are able to influence the instructions they receive so that they may carry out instructions without violation of conscience. When there has been a clash between instructions and conscience, a few have resigned: Evan Luard and Peter Mansfield resigned from the British diplomatic service over the Suez affair in 1956, and Lord Caradon resigned once over Britain's policy towards Southern Africa, and threatened to do so on more than one occasion subsequently.

The difficulty for the diplomat is that diplomacy depends on compromise, but how can one distinguish between a concession of marginal importance, a sacrifice of vital national interest, and a violation of personal conscience?

Friends often ask for an enhancement of the moral element in international decision-making, and they are quite right to do so. At the same time, we should recognize that for the harassed foreign minister or ambassador, the distinction between the pragmatic and the ethical is often blurred. The most effective Quakers in international affairs are not those who think of ministers and diplomats as knaves or fools, but those who enter with sympathy into the painful dilemmas and difficult choices which national decision-makers confront. Sometimes this becomes almost a pastoral role.

I recall one diplomat who had served as a courier for the underground during the second world war. He had been captured by the Nazis, tortured, and had disclosed the names of some of his colleagues in the underground movement. These colleagues had then been arrested, and some had been executed. After the war, the man we knew had decided to devote his life to the cause of world peace, but instead of starting a new peace organization, he had joined his country's diplomatic service. When he felt uneasy about his instructions, he would come round to Quaker house in New York in the hope that a quiet confidential conversation with the Quaker staff would lead to the discovery of a formula of which both his government and his conscience would approve.

We know, of course, that some espionage activities are conducted under diplomatic cover, and several diplomats who have regularly participated in activities at William Penn House have been expelled from the United Kingdom for 'activities incompatible with their diplomatic status', as it is put in official communiqués. The British security service has shown sporadic interest in our meetings for diplomats. Twice in forty years I have been approached by foreign diplomats with the tentative suggestion that I should provide information in exchange for unspecified rewards.

It is difficult to know what to do about occasional gifts from diplomatic friends. When Brenda and I were new at Quaker House in New York, we received a few Christmas presents of national handicrafts from diplomatic friends. Gradually, over the years, the gifts became more lavish. It would have been churlish to have refused all gifts, but we soon became embarrassed by extravagant Christmas presents. We decided to report all gifts to the executive secretary of AFSC, and it was suggested to us that when the presents came in bottled form, they should be distributed among staff and committee. In sending 'thank you' notes to the senders, we explained that this was what we had done. One Christmas, after our return to London, we received a large crate of oranges from a Middle Eastern embassy (reported to the Recording Clerk and shared with Quaker colleagues). Shortly thereafter, the ambassador of that country's chief rival in the Middle East, expelled from Britain in 1986, began the practice of giving us a bottle of wine each Christmas, always handed in at the reception desk at Friends House. Needless to say, in none of these cases did the receipt of gifts affect our attitudes to the policies of the countries concerned.

After Yugoslavia broke with the rest of the Soviet bloc in 1948, the Cominform started to allege that Yugoslavia was hosting US military bases and was preparing military aggression against its Communist neighbours. The Yugoslav Committee for the Defence of Peace invited foreign peace organizations to send delegations to their country to see for themselves that these allegations were false. The British National Peace Council was the first (and I believe the only) peace organization to accept the invitation.

Before leaving Britain, we obtained from the BBC Monitoring Service the texts of all Cominform broadcasts naming specific places in Yugoslavia where US bases were alleged to exist or war-like preparations were said to be taking place. On arriving in Belgrade, our Yugoslav hosts handed us a proposed itinerary. We quickly saw that it did not contain any of the dozen locations mentioned in Cominform broadcasts. We pointed out the omissions to our Yugoslav friends, who were clearly taken aback and deeply embarrassed. Our hosts said that they would have to consult higher authorities, and the next morning they said it would be quite impossible for us to visit the named places and regions as they were all in 15 km security zones along Yugoslavia's frontiers, from which foreigners were excluded. We then said, in the friendliest way possible, that we would accept their proposed itinerary and would report on our return to Britain on what we had seen and the fact that we had not been able to visit any of the places and regions named in Cominform propaganda. Later in the day, we were given a revised schedule including all but one of the twelve places we had asked to visit. The exception was the island of Vis which was, however, visited by the AFSC delegation about ten days after our stay in Yugoslavia. The unpublished diary of the American mission in the AFSC archives in Philadelphia includes the following: 'All suggestion that Vis is a centre of aggressive preparation, Yugoslav or foreign, is palpably absurd.' As far as the delegation from the British National Peace Council was concerned, in not a single case did we find evidence of US military bases, not even an empty coke bottle or a discarded US cigarette packet, and in none of the areas where Yugoslavia was alleged to be planning aggression against its Communist neighbours did we find any preparations for offensive military action.[174]

The point of recalling this episode is that thirty-nine years after our visit, I learned that one of my colleagues in the National Peace Council delegation had been an agent of the British secret intelligence service.[175]

CONSCIENTIOUS OBJECTION TO MILITARY SERVICE

One of the purposes stated in the UN Charter is to promote respect for human rights and fundamental freedoms for all (Articles 1.3 and 55.c), and the Universal Declaration of Human Rights states that freedom of religion includes the right to manifest religion 'in teaching, practice, worship and observance' (Article 18). Friends have regarded the right

to refuse military service on grounds of conscience as a basic mani-
festation of religious belief and observance, a right that should be
expressly recognized by the appropriate UN organ.

In 1949, Service Civil International submitted to the UN Human
Rights Commission a statement to the effect that anyone whose
religious beliefs or deep convictions forbid him to participate directly
or indirectly in armed conflict should be guaranteed the right to perform a civilian alternative service. This was circulated to the Commission at the request of the Lebanon, but no action was taken. In 1950, a
statement in the name of the Friends World Committee for Consultation was submitted to the UN Human Rights Commission urging
that the right of conscientious objection to military service should be
recognized in the Covenant on Human Rights then in course of preparation, and the Philippines proposed the inclusion in the Covenant of
the following provision:

> Persons who conscientiously object to war as being contrary to their
> religion shall be exempt from military service.

After a brief discussion, the proposal of the Philippines was
withdrawn.[176]

There was some division among the Quaker agencies as to whether
further action should be taken on the matter. It was felt by some that
this was a subject about which Friends had special experience and
competence, and that this should be made available to the UN. Others
felt that the FWCC's consultative status at the UN should not be used
to pursue a matter which could be represented as being of a narrowly
selfish interest to pacifists. When I examined the files of the Quaker UN
offices in 1955, the main impression I received was of 'indecision'.

In 1956, however, a new opportunity arose to establish the right of
conscientious objection in a UN document, after the UN Sub-Commis-
sion on Discrimination and Minorities had requested one of its members, Arcot Krishnaswami of India, to prepare a report on
discrimination regarding religious rights and practices. Krishnaswami's report was based on factual monographs about government
policy in more than eighty countries, information from the secretariats
of the UN and the specialized agencies, and submissions from non-
governmental organizations. The Quaker UN Office in New York submitted to Krishnaswami a written statement in the name of the FWCC,
and I discussed the matter with him informally on a number of occa-

sions. We were pleased that he included in his report a short section on freedom from performing military service when this was incompatible with religion or belief, but dismayed at the limited and in some respects damaging character of what he had to say. He reported that government policy on the issue varied from country to country 'according to circumstances and the state of public opinion'. Some countries did not exempt COs, some granted exemption to ministers of religion or other specified categories, while some granted exemption from combatant or non-combatant service to those willing to perform a civilian alternative.

So far, so good. But Krishnaswami went on to say that some COs were unwilling to perform 'any services which are even remotely connected with a military effort; in the present circumstances [1960] hardly any society can afford to recognize this stand.' Krishnaswami was here confusing the position of those absolutists who demanded unconditional exemption from military service on grounds of conscience and those COs, perhaps the majority, who were willing to perform alternative service so long as it was not directly in support of the war effort. But worse was to come, for Krishnaswami went on to state that should a CO refuse any service connected with the war effort but be willing to perform alternative civilian service, 'the population of the country as a whole may feel that any exemption creates a privilege entailing discriminatory treatment of others.' In other words, to recognize the right of conscientious objection could be regarded as discrimination against non-COs. Needless to say, this argument would have undermined much of what Krishnaswami wrote elsewhere in his report about religious discrimination.[177]

This story had a happy ending, however, for after intensive efforts by the Quaker UN staff in Geneva over many years, the UN Human Rights Commission decided in 1987 that 'conscientious objection to military service' is 'a legitimate exercise of the right to freedom of thought, conscience and religion.'[178] It still remains to convert this opinion of a UN organ into action in Member States.

THE REPRESENTATION OF CHINA
One of the most difficult issues we had to handle when I was in the Quaker office at the UN concerned China's UN seat. The Chinese delegation at the founding conference at San Francisco in 1945 had included a Communist (Tung Pi-wu), and the Charter had named 'the

Republic of China' as one of the permanent members of the Security Council (Article 23.1). After the victory of the Communists in the Chinese civil war, the question arose as to whether China's seat at the UN should be occupied by a representative of the People's Republic of China or of the Nationalist régime in Taiwan. It was because of the failure of the Security Council to expel the Chinese Nationalist delegation that the Soviet Union boycotted the Security Council from 13 January to 31 July 1950, during which time the Korean war broke out.

We faced two difficulties over this issue, one internal to the Quaker family, and one arising from an unusual procedure adopted by the United States in the UN General Assembly. The Quaker difficulty was simply that Friends were for a time divided on the issue. Virtually all non-American Friends and the majority of American Friends on the Atlantic and Pacific coasts favoured universality of UN Membership and therefore thought that, on balance, the People's Republic of China should occupy China's seat at the UN. The quite numerous Friends in the American Middle West, or a majority of them, took the view that Nationalist China should not be deprived of its UN seat. A minute of the AFSC's UN Committee in 1958 recognized the problem for the staff, but noted that

> those who have most closely followed UN activities over the years . . . feel that the principle of universal membership of the UN is a sound one, and tend to agree that some arrangement needs to be worked out whereby the Peking government could be represented.[179]

The procedural difficulty at the UN was that the United States submitted a proposal each year from 1951–60 either to postpone or not to consider the question of Chinese representation. As this was a procedural matter and therefore in terms of Article 18 of the UN Charter, not an 'important' question, a simple majority rather than a two-thirds vote sufficed.

During the 1960s, as the Chinese Nationalists abandoned the hope of re-taking the Mainland and as the absence of China from the UN became more absurd, Quaker opinion began to swing in favour of giving China's seat to the People's Republic. After intensive consultations among Quaker agencies in 1969, it was decided that the relevant Quaker programmes (the two UN offices, Quaker international affairs representatives, the Conferences for Diplomats) would make an intensive effort over the next two years in favour of seating China at the United Nations. A publication was produced showing the voting between 1951 and 1969 on the various aspects of Chinese representation, and identifying the floating voters (countries that had usually abstained or had changed their votes).[180] Quaker persuasive powers were directed at these floating voters in the places around the world where Friends had influence, and one remarkable Quaker conference for diplomats dealing exclusively with the issue was held in Austria in 1970.

There were, of course, governments and other non-governmental agencies that were also working on the issue. In 1971, the UN General Assembly voted by 76 votes to 35 'to restore all its rights to the People's Republic of China . . . and to expel forthwith the representatives of Chiang Kai-shek.'[181]

THE LAVON AFFAIR

I would like to illustrate one of the problems of Quaker international work by describing an event relating to the Middle East in 1954–55. The difficult question is: in what circumstances should Friends make representations to foreign governments regarding named victims of oppression?

On 16 December 1954, a senior Israeli diplomat came to lunch at Quaker House, New York. In the course of conversation, our Israeli friend invoked Quaker help in connexion with some innocent young Egyptian Jews who were being tried in Cairo on trumped-up charges of espionage. If they were adjudged guilty, and particularly if any of them were sentenced to death, this would be a grave setback for prospects for peace in the area.

Friends are, in fact, often asked to intercede in this way: the matter had come up in our East-West work in London. I had taken the line that, before deciding to act, we should always ask three questions.

1. Is the action complained of an infraction of some *international* obligation of the country concerned, such as a violation of a Human Rights treaty?
2. Is the victim known personally to Quaker workers?
3. Are we sure of the relevant facts?

Even if all three answers were 'no', we might still feel it right to act; but we should always ask the three questions.

In the 1954 case, all three answers were 'no', and I expressed to Quaker colleagues my uneasiness about acting too precipitately without further information. I was, however, very much of a novice in the Quaker UN office in New York, having arrived only three months previously. Moreover, the director of the office (Elmore Jackson) was on leave of absence, and the acting director was as inexperienced as I was in such matters.

At the time of the Israeli request, there were two things about this incident that we did not know. The first was that the Israelis had invoked our help not because of any special Quaker qualities: it was part of an intensive world-wide campaign to secure clemency for the people on trial in Cairo. Gideon Rafael, who was coordinating matters in Israel's Foreign Office, has since written:

> We decided to activate all available personal connections and public bodies who might influence Nasser. Members of parliament, representatives of the Church, human rights organizations and friendly governments intervened in Cairo.

Among those who were particularly active in this way were Maurice Orbach (a Labour MP) and Roger Baldwin (Chairman of the International League for the Rights of Man).[182]

As far as Friends were concerned, we were greatly influenced by the fact that sentences of guilty, and any executions, would undoubtedly obstruct the peace process. The chairman of the AFSC's UN Committee raised the matter with Egyptian officials in New York, and four Friends (including Clarence Pickett) discussed the matter with the wife of the Egyptian ambassador in Washington, expressing in particular the concern of Friends that justice would be administered in such a way as not to increase tension in the region. Israeli diplomats were informed of the action taken, and appreciative letters were received from two of them.[183] Two of the accused were executed on 31 January 1955, six were sentenced to long terms of imprisonment, and two were acquitted. One committed suicide during the course of the trial.

The second thing we did not know at the time did not become apparent until some years later. In September 1960, there was a domestic political crisis in Israel, leading the following January to the resignation of David Ben-Gurion and his government. At first it was thought that the cabinet crisis was about Ben-Gurion's high-handed style, but eventually it became known that the row was over Ben-Gurion's refusal to accept the report of a committee of inquiry into a security operation that had misfired while Pinhas Lavon was Minister of Defence. The persons described to us as innocent Egyptian Jews were, in fact, Israeli agents. Their mission had been to sabotage US and British installations in Egypt in an attempt to discredit the Nasser régime and stir up bad feeling between the West and Egypt.

The Lavon Affair, as it is now called , came into the news again in 1971 as a result of an exchange of prisoners arranged by the UN representative, ambassador Gunnar Jarring. One of the saboteurs released by the Egyptians was Victorine Marcelle Ninno. As she was 33 years old in 1971, she must have been 16 at the time of her arrest in 1954. Miss Ninno was married in November 1971, and the Israeli Prime Minister (Golda Meir) gave the bride away.

CONFERENCES FOR DIPLOMATS
This was one of the most innovative and exciting Quaker peace programmes since the second world war. It arose out of seminars which the AFSC had initiated in Washington in order to bring the 'findings' of the social sciences to the attention of US policy-makers. The founders of the programme recognized that diplomats are agents of the governments they represent, but it was believed that, within these constraints, they could play a key role in relieving international tension.

When British Friends were consulted about the first Conference for Diplomats in 1952, virtually all regarded it as a ridiculous and impractical idea. Not for the first time, Friends in Britain thought that AFSC had embarked hastily on an ill-conceived project. Diplomats, it was said, had no influence on national decision-making. They were far too busy to take a fortnight from work or holiday for a conference focussed on vague Quakerly concerns. If spouses and children came, how would they occupy themselves? And would not the Foreign Offices think that we had a hidden agenda, that our real purpose was to convert the participants to Quakerism?

The British Foreign Office was equally sceptical, and no British diplomats participated in the first conference.

But the AFSC had, in fact, hit on a brilliant idea. The first conference was an outstanding success, and I never heard that any of the 92 subsequent conferences were regarded by the Quaker sponsors as unsatisfactory. Much to my regret, the programme was terminated in 1976, but shorter conferences for diplomats and other decision-makers are still run on an *ad hoc* basis by the two Quaker offices at the UN and by some regional Quaker representatives.

The residential conferences had four main purposes.

1. To reinforce the commitment of diplomats to ethical principles and values, regardless of their own ideology or religion.
2. To open up for discussion the findings of social science, peace and conflict research, and other disciplines bearing on contemporary diplomacy.
3. To raise issues of special Quaker concern (e.g. refugee problems, disarmament, mediation, human rights).
4. To facilitate human contact across political barriers.

The programme was administered by the AFSC but, from 1960, co-sponsored by British Friends. The first conference was held in Europe in 1952, and the programme was later extended to Asia and, in modified form, to Africa. A conference for parliamentarians was held in Switzerland in 1959, and the founding conference of the International Peace Research Association took place in Switzerland under Quaker auspices in 1963. The directory of past participants issued in 1976 showed that over 1,400 diplomats who had attended Quaker conferences could be found in 155 cities around the world.

The programme was based on the following practical considerations.

Location. A comfortable but not sumptuous building of which we had the exclusive use, preferably sufficiently remote from the capital or nearest UN office so that the participants would not be tempted to wander off on official business during the course of the conference. Thirty-three conferences between 1952 and 1976 were held during the summer vacation at a girls' boarding school overlooking Lac Leman in Switzerland, and eight in Eastern Europe.

Participants were mid-career diplomats and their families, plus consultants and a few Quakers. We made it clear in advance, and again during the opening session, that the conferences were private and off-the-record. The media would not be present, and neither the Quakers nor the participants would issue public reports of what had been said.

In theory, the participants were there in their personal capacities and not to speak for their governments, but there was a good deal of variation in the extent to which this was achieved. The only participant from a Communist state at the first conference was from Yugoslavia, but beginning in 1957, there was a respectable contingent from Eastern Europe at each conference.

We made a considerable effort to recruit Chinese diplomats, but without success. In 1969, we invited a diplomat from the German Democratic Republic, leading to a boycott of the conference by all NATO members except the Netherlands and Norway. It was argued, on the one hand, that by inviting East German participation, we were only acting in accordance with a reality that the rest of the world recognized four years later. The contrary view was that one purpose of the conferences was to achieve understanding across barriers and that it was futile to organize a conference in Europe from which one bloc was largely absent.[184]

At one of the early conferences, a diplomat from a country that had been occupied during the second world war told me that he was willing to have normal personal relations with his diplomatic colleagues other than those from the Axis powers which had caused so much suffering to his country. One afternoon, on the tennis courts, quite by chance, he was drawn as partner with a diplomat from an Axis country—and they won. Gradually a friendship developed between the two, and they discovered that they had been in the same region during the closing stages of the war, one in the occupying army and the other as an underground fighter. But they also discovered how similar had been their experiences—cold, hunger, loneliness, fear, and so on. They became firm friends.

At a conference in the 1970s, at which both Arabs and Israelis were present, one of the Arab diplomats (now a distinguished ambassador) told the conference director that he was unwilling to have anything to do with any Israeli participant. For a few days, he boycotted his discussion group, but eventually relented. During the conference, his two children found themselves playing football with the two children of an Israeli diplomat, not realizing that this was not *comme il faut*. Fortunately, the parents did not intervene. At the party on the final evening, the Arab diplomat invited the beautiful daughter of an Israeli participant to be his dancing partner.[185] There are many such episodes in Quaker memories and archives.

Some former participants have gone on to play distinguished roles in international affairs. James C. Jonah of Sierra Leone (1965) is Under-Secretary-General at the UN for Political Affairs. Yasushi Akashi of Japan (1965, 1966, and 1971) is in charge of the UN operation in Cambodia. Ismat Kittani, an Iraqi Kurd (1965, 1966, and 1969), is in charge of the UN operation in Somalia.* Edouard Brunner of Switzerland (1965 and 1971) was in 1991 appointed to succeed Gunnar Jarring as UN Special Representative for the Middle East. Chief Emeka Anyaoku of Nigeria (1974) is Secretary-General of the Commonwealth. Enrique Ros of Argentina (1967 and 1970) was his country's chief negotiator with the UK during the Falklands/Malvinas war in 1982. Noel Dorr of Ireland (1962 and 1968) is Secretary of his country's Department of Foreign Affairs. Amre Moussa (1963) is the Egyptian Foreign Minister. Many other examples could be cited.

Programme. The first conference lasted a fortnight. Later ones were cut down to 8 to 10 days. Each evening there was a major address by a consultant. In the morning there were two sessions in small groups, chaired by a past participant. The afternoons were free for recreation, excursions, and optional sessions: there was often a spontaneous demand from the participants for an optional session on Quakerism. We had a fifteen-minute meeting for worship each day, and many of the diplomats joined us at least once.

The over-all theme of the conferences was National Interest and International Responsibility, expressing in pointed fashion the dilemma faced by diplomats in their day-to-day work, but providing scope for a wide range of topics.

We always stressed that it was not the purpose of the conferences to deal with current issues, but the conference in Czechoslovakia in 1967 began on the same day as the June war in the Middle East: under pressure from some of the participants, we inserted an optional session on what had to be done to remove Arab and Israeli grievances.

Occasionally, when there was substantial agreement on some issue, we would be asked to have this put in writing and submitted to the final session for approval. We always resisted this, for we thought that if we agreed, some participants would come the following year with draft resolutions, and time would then be spent negotiating about words rather than in listening to and learning from each other.

*In April 1993, the UN Secretary-General appointed Kittani his Special Envoy for Tajikistan.

The London-based diplomats from the first conference in 1952 decided to hold a reunion the following winter, and there thus came into existence the so-called Clarens Group of former participants. Later, other diplomats, usually those who had had previous associations with Quaker work, were invited in order to achieve a better geographical and ideological balance. The London programme moved to William Penn House in 1962. It has continued now for more than forty years.

QUAKER PEACE-MAKING
Quaker witness against war and for peace now takes four main forms, though these are not sharply differentiated, and one may merge into another: humanitarian service (to which I have already referred), advocacy, reconciliation, and mediation. In giving examples of reconciliation and mediation, I have found it necessary to avoid referring to recent activities in order not to embarrass people who are still active in public life.

(i) Advocacy. This may take the form of demonstrations or other kinds of public witness or the expression of Quaker principles and policies, orally or in writing, to the general public or to national or international decision-makers. Much of this takes place at the local level, when individual Friends or Meetings write to members of the government, MPs, or newspapers about matters about which they are concerned. It also takes place internationally in the capitals, at the UN offices in Geneva and New York, and by Quaker representatives in various regions.

Friends sometimes describe this process as Speaking Truth to Power, believing that the expression comes from early Friends. The AFSC published a pamphlet in 1955 in which it was stated that the title, *Speak Truth to Power*, was 'taken from a charge given to Eighteenth Century Friends' (p.iv). This was affirmed in good faith, but in fact seems not to have been correct.

Stephen Cary tells me that he first heard the expression at a meeting of the AFSC working party, of which he was chair, at Haverford College in July 1954.

> We were in the midst of drafting a document on the relevance of pacifism in the modern world which was later published under that title [*Speak Truth to Power*], and one morning Milton Mayer opened

our working session with the announcement that he had our title: Speak Truth to Power. Everyone present thought it was a great suggestion and pressed Milton on where he'd dug it up. He couldn't recall, beyond saying he thought it was an old Quaker phrase. Since then a lot of people have tried to identify its source, without success. No less a Quaker historian than Henry Cadbury turned his attention to it [but] had no luck in his researches. And there the matter stands to this day.[186]

It is a convenient phrase, even if of recent lineage, and it has in recent years spread beyond the borders of Quakerdom.

Quaker advocacy sometimes takes a quite generalized form: the protection of the natural environment, the need for radical disarmament, promotion of a humane penal policy on a world-wide basis, the protection of human rights, the needs of refugees and displaced persons, respect for international law, and so on. At other times, Quaker advocacy may be quite specific. The mission to the Soviet Union in 1951 presented Yaacov Malik with seven proposals for easing Cold War tensions. The following year, we presented to Selwyn Lloyd at the Foreign Office a four-point plan to end the fighting in Korea.[187] One point was of a general nature: Friends asked that 'all Governments' should urge the media to exercise restraint and not impute evil motives to the other side. The three substantive points, concerning the deadlock in the armistice negotiations at Panmunjom, were as follows.

Firstly, Friends urged that a mutual cease-fire be effected in Korea on the conditions already agreed, leaving the prisoner-of-war issue to be resolved later. This was suggested so as to release the Unified Command negotiators from 'their exacting and exhausting labours': fresh minds could then be brought to bear on outstanding problems. Friends admitted that a cease-fire without resolving the POW issue would necessarily lead to some delay in the release of those POWs who were willing to be repatriated, but it would mean an earlier end to carnage and destruction.

Secondly, on the question whether POWs should be sent home against their will, Friends admitted that this was required by strict adherence to the letter of the Geneva Convention. On the other hand, the statement continued, the drafters of the Convention had hardly anticipated a situation in which some prisoners might be reluctant to be repatriated.* We went on to say that after the second world war, Quaker relief workers had been 'profoundly disturbed at being involved in forced repatriation which ignored the fears of individuals': this was a reference to the experience of a Friends Relief Service team at Goslar in Germany in 1946, when East European nationals were sent unwillingly to countries under Communist control. The statement on Korea suggested that re-screening and release of POWs should be put in the hands of a commission composed of Asian governments or 'a mixed commission of two appointed by each side'. The problem should be resolved in accordance with the spirit rather than the letter of the Geneva Convention, and prisoners rejecting repatriation should be 'given asylum' in areas where they would not be used in any further fighting.

Our final point was to commend 'the good offices of India'.

Three things are of interest about these points. First, although we did not know it at the time, our second point was similar to a proposal that Mexico had submitted to the United States a few days after our statement had been finalized but before it was sent to the British Government. It seems likely, though we will never know for sure, that these two parallel but similar proposals contributed to the decision of the UN General Assembly later in 1952 and the conclusion of the Korean armistice the following year.

Secondly, we suggested that the principle of free choice should take precedence over the strict letter of an international treaty. Friends have always taken the position that an immoral law should not be obeyed, but our Geneva staff had raised no objection to the ramifications of the Geneva Convention for the protection of prisoners-of-war when it was adopted in 1949, probably because Friends had not foreseen a situation in which POWs would refuse to go home when hostilities ended.

Thirdly, Selwyn Lloyd told us, for our own most confidential information only, that our first proposal would probably be acceptable to HMG. We did not report this precise piece of information to Meeting for Sufferings but simply gave 'an encouraging account' of the interview. It is fortunate that we did not allow Lloyd's position to leak out,

*This was not correct: a proposal by Austria that a POW should be entitled to ask for transfer to a country other than his own had been submitted at the conference which led to the adoption of the Geneva Convention in 1949, but was rejected. It could be argued that Friends could hardly have been expected to know the precise details of the 1949 negotiations on the Geneva Conventions. On the other hand, we might have carried more weight if we had checked the facts before making a categorical assertion on such a crucial issue.

for when Lloyd reached New York for the UN General Assembly a few weeks later, he was subject to intense pressure from Dean Acheson, the US Secretary of State, who himself was under equally intense pressure from the Pentagon, the China Lobby, and the Republican Party. Recently declassified documents reveal that on 3 November, Lloyd sent a personal and confidential letter to Anthony Eden saying that it would be highly dangerous to stop the fighting in Korea without a provision for the repatriation of 'our' POWs.[188]

Did our intervention make any difference? This was a question some Friends asked at the time, but we were never able to give a definitive answer. The Quaker proposals found a place in the Indian resolution on POWs during the 1952 session of the UN General Assembly, which itself provided the basis for dealing with the problem in the armistice agreement the following year. But in the event, the armistice provisions on POWs were wrecked by the obstructive tactics of the two sides in Korea. All I can say forty years later is that I am glad we put forward constructive proposals at a critical juncture in a tragic war.

An interesting hybrid between advocacy and reconciliation was initiated by the AFSC in 1968, in association with British Quaker Committees, the Canadian Friends Service Committee, and the Friends World Committee for Consultation. This was the study *Search for Peace in the Middle East*.[189] This booklet contained a factual description of the positions of the main parties, suggested some principles for a peace settlement, and outlined an expression of Quaker concern and hope. But the innovative aspect of the exercise was that the study went through nineteen drafts, and each draft was taken by the Quaker representatives in the Middle East (Paul and Jean Johnson) to their contacts on the two sides and comments were invited. The Israelis and the Arabs were careful to draw attention to even minor factual errors or misrepresentations of their respective viewpoints, but in searching diligently for these, they read, learned, and perhaps inwardly digested, the point of view of the other side.

One word of warning is needed about the relationship of advocacy to reconciliation and mediation. At a critical stage of Quaker mediation in the Nigeria-Biafra war, one of our Quaker committees in London called on the British Government to stop sending arms to Federal Nigeria, and at about the same time, the AFSC placed an advertisement in the *New York Times* appealing in rather purple prose for funds for relief in Biafra and Vietnam. Not surprisingly, it was difficult for Quaker mediators to persuade the Federal Nigerians that Friends were impartial.[190] Contradictions of this kind are probably unavoidable, but damage can be limited if those concerned know in advance when they are likely to occur.

(ii) Reconciliation. This involves a long-term, open-ended effort to build bridges of understanding between peoples—what is sometimes called (by me) people-to-people diplomacy. As Richard Ullmann stressed, reconciliation is about people, not policies.[191] It includes all kinds of contact—visits and missions, conferences, exchanges of personnel, and various kinds of written communication. Reconciliation is especially needed when our own country is at loggerheads with other states or entities: with Afrikaners after the Anglo-Boer War, with Germany after the two world wars, with the Communist states after 1945. Reconciliation may also be needed when two communities within one state are in dispute or conflict and external Friends exercise third party reconciliation, as Friends have done in Northern Ireland and Sri Lanka.

An interesting example of reconciliation, not under official Quaker auspices but significantly Quaker in personnel, was the India Conciliation Group. Carl Heath chaired the Group, and Alexander Wilson was treasurer. Agatha Harrison, the secretary, joined Friends in 1940. Other Quaker members at various times included Horace Alexander, Gerald Bailey, Percy Bartlett, Hilda Clark, Joan Mary Fry, Marion Parmoor, and Edith Pye. Among the non-Quaker members were C. F. Andrews, Muriel Lester, and Maud Royden. I was a very junior member from 1947 until the Group ended in 1950.[192]

The Group came into existence in 1931, when Gandhi was in London for the Round Table Conference on India's political future. Its main function was to act as a channel of communication and interpretation between the India Office in London and the Viceroy in India, on the one hand, and Gandhi, Nehru, and other leaders of the Indian Congress Party, on the other. After about 1940, the Group attempted to perform a similar role with Jinnah and the Muslim League, but not as satisfactorily. Agatha Harrison always wished for more face-to-face contacts between British and Indian leaders, but I have often speculated that her reconciling intermediary role led to greater mutual understanding than direct meetings would have done.

Professor Hugh Tinker, a distinguished scholar of South Asian

Agatha Harrison and Horace Alexander, members of the India Conciliation Group.

affairs, has written a perceptive article on the Group's role over the twenty years of its existence. He points out that the members were self-appointed and self-selected, and that they all came from the same social class—'enlightened professional and managerial folk.' The Group stood between the powerless and the power-holders, writes Tinker, and had to deal with two entirely different sets of expectations. He believes that those in the middle can never satisfy both parties, and that this tends to lead to factionalism within the intermediaries. The India Conciliation Group, however, was 'never reduced to internecine strife', though from time to time, one or other member would raise pointed questions about its role. (I thought that some of my colleagues under-estimated the factors making for Indian partition.)

We tended to give British imperialism an acceptable face, and thus encouraged the forces of moderation in India, but our influence on British policy seems to Tinker to have been marginal. On only one occasion did the Group succeed in modifying British policy. In 1932, the British Prime Minister, Ramsay Macdonald announced that a new constitution for India would be introduced in which the *harijans* (untouchables) would vote on a separate electoral roll. Gandhi, who was in prison at the time, believed that this would increase rather than reduce tension between caste Hindus and the *harijans*. On 13 September, he announced that he would begin a fast unto death in a week's time if the decision were not reversed. Gandhi and the *harijan* leader, B. R. Ambedkar, then negotiated an agreement (the Poona Pact) whereby seats would be reserved for *harijans*, but voting would be by the whole Hindu electorate. Gandhi then called off his fast.

When news of this reached Britain, the India Conciliation Group decided to urge MacDonald to amend his plan. C. F. Andrews was despatched to Chequers, and MacDonald quickly agreed to change course. The India Conciliation Group organized a national day of prayer for India.

Hugh Tinker considers that, while the India Conciliation Group had only limited success in modifying *public policy*, it certainly was able to affect *attitudes* on both sides. This is confirmed for the Indian side when, in 1952, Sir Girja Bajpai, secretary-general of the Indian Foreign Ministry, told the US ambassador that Nehru was 'still considerably influenced by correspondence from [a] group of extremely confused Quakers in London whom he had known years ago, among them an elderly lady named Agatha Harrison.'[193]

We cannot now know if Bajpai was accurately reflecting Nehru's view. Certainly Nehru and other leaders of the Indian Congress Party welcomed the activities of the India Conciliation Group before Indian independence in 1947. Nehru was, however, exasperated that some of the same people, now wearing Quaker hats, kept asking him to mediate over the Korean war (1950–53). I recall one painful meeting between Friends and Nehru in London in, I think, 1952 when, at a Quaker suggestion that he should mediate, Nehru retorted petulantly, 'why not do your own mediating?'

Another example of reconciliation arose from the action of Swedish Friends. On the initiative of Elsa Cedegren in 1947, Swedish Friends had promoted the idea of a tour of Swedish social institutions by a group of Soviet citizens and Quakers from Britain, the United States, and Sweden. Friends in Sweden made an approach to the Soviet embassy in Stockholm in 1950, which suggested that a letter be sent to the Soviet Peace Committee. This was done at once, and again in 1951, 1952, and 1953. These repeated approaches were fruitless, until the last week of July 1953, when a message was received from the Soviet embassy to say that five Russians would be arriving in Stockholm the following Friday afternoon. I was one of five Anglo-American Friends recruited at short notice to take part in this innovative venture. When the Russians arrived, we found that four of them were pastors of the Evangelical-Baptist Church: the general secretary and vice-president of the Baptist Union (who had met members of the Quaker mission to the Soviet Union in 1951)[194] and the bishops of Leningrad (St. Petersburg) and Kiev. The fifth member of the delegation was an interpreter from the Soviet Academy of Sciences, whom one suspicious Quaker thought was a watch-dog for the Soviet secret police. Apparently the Soviet Foreign Ministry had passed the Swedish invitation to the Soviet Peace Committee, which had decided that Baptists were the most suitable people to talk with Quakers.[195]

This was an interesting time in Soviet affairs. Stalin had died five months previously, and G. M. Malenkov was the new Soviet Prime Minister, to be replaced by Khrushchev a few weeks after the Swedish venture. The group of Western Quakers and Soviet visitors travelled around the country in four separate cars, so the interpreter was not present at all the conversations. I usually travelled in the same car as the general secretary of the Russian Baptist Union, Aleksander Vasilievic Karev.

Russian Baptist pastors and their interpreter in Sweden in 1953. Aleksander Vasilievic Karev is on the left.

The Quakers had agreed in advance not to publish a report of the conversations so as not to inhibit frankness of expression. The Russian Baptists, as was their right, published a detailed diary in their journal *Bratsky Vietnik* (Fraternal Bulletin). They were clearly intrigued by our daily meetings for worship, many of which were entirely silent. The issue that the Russians raised persistently was why Friends did not take part in the massive conferences of the World Peace Council (the Partizans of Peace), one assembly of which had been held in Vienna the previous December. According to the Russian account of this conversation, the Quakers regarded the Partizans of Peace as having as one of its aims the dissemination of Communist ideas, and this the Russians hotly denied. When we spoke of the need for increasing understanding and trust between peoples, the Baptists replied that the more pressing task was to avoid war. 'When a house is on fire [said one of our Russian friends] the most useful person isn't the one who convenes a conference on methods of avoiding fires, but the one who organizes fire-fighters. We Christians in the Soviet Union are peace-fighters.'

At the final session, we all agreed on the text of a brief factual declaration to be issued by Swedish Friends. This used characteristic Quaker jargon: the meetings had been private and informal, discussions had been frank and friendly, we would discuss in our countries further measure to achieve lasting peace.[196]

The further measure I agreed to pursue was the possibility of an inter-Church delegation from Britain to the Soviet Union. I had been co-opted to the Board of International Affairs of the British Council of Churches the previous year, but the BCC was not yet ready in 1953 for anything as adventurous as a mission to Moscow. After consulting the Quaker East-West Relations Group, I raised the matter with the Council of Christian Action, which approved the idea with enthusiasm. I therefore wrote to Karev of the Baptists and Metropolitan Nikolai of the Orthodox Church, and after a short delay, they invited Christian Action to send an inter-Church delegation to the Soviet Union for private discussions on the contribution of Christians to the cause of world peace.

The Christian Action delegation visited the Soviet Union in May 1955. The group decided to have no set agenda for discussion and to make no attempt to arrive at agreed resolutions, 'but simply to get to know one another and to learn of one another's problems.' The delegates spent most of the time with Baptist and Orthodox leaders, but they also visited a comprehensive school and the Moscow State Uni-

132   *Swarthmore Lecture 1993*

versity. They were impressed with the spirit of ecumenical cooperation among Soviet Church leaders, arising largely from their involvement in the activities of the Soviet Peace Committee. 'They obviously took the World Peace Movement at its face value, being quite unconscious of the doubts which are felt about the purpose of this movement outside the Soviet Union.'[197]

Quaker efforts for reconciliation have, of course, been directed to the Arab-Israel conflict through practical service and the presence in the region of Quaker representatives. Among the residential conferences with Arab and Israeli participants were those held in France in 1974, in Turkey in 1976 and 1977, in Cyprus and in Greece in 1990, and in Switzerland in 1975, 1989, and 1991.

Perhaps the most remarkable conference of this type was one for Jews, Christians, and Muslims, held in Rome under the joint auspices of the American Universities Field Staff and the Quaker service agencies. The idea for this originated in 1970 with the Rt. Rev. George Appleton, then the Anglican Archbishop in Jerusalem. He discussed the proposal with me in London and then with Paul and Jean Johnson, the Quaker representatives in the Middle East. It took two years for Appleton's idea to materialize, but in 1972, twenty-five senior representatives of the three Faiths from eight countries met, with Appleton in the chair, to consider 'A Spiritual Charter for Jerusalem'. Teddy Kollek, Mayor of Jerusalem, was present as a consultant. During the course of one session, I commented 'It is people and not places that are holy', and was immediately attacked by adherents of all three Faiths![198]

(iii) Mediation. There is one pitfall in our Quaker use of the word 'mediation'. What Quakers call 'mediation' is now called by diplomats and international lawyers 'good offices'. The UN *Handbook on the Peaceful Settlement of Disputes between States* defines 'good offices' as follows:

When States parties to a dispute are unable to settle it directly between themselves, a third party may offer his good offices as a means of preventing further deterioration of the dispute and as a method of facilitating efforts towards a peaceful settlement of the dispute. Such an offer of good offices, whether upon the initiative of the third party in question or upon the request of one or more of the parties to the dispute, is subject to acceptance by all the parties to the dispute . . .*

*The intermediary may be a State, a group of States, or a single individual.

Mediation, on the other hand, has one different feature in that the parties agree that the intermediary may not only exercise good offices but may also propose terms of settlement. *The UN Handbook* puts it like this.

> Mediation is a method of peaceful settlement of an international dispute where a third party intervenes to reconcile the claims of the contending parties *and to advance his own proposals aimed at a mutually acceptable compromise solution* [my italics].*[199]

Each mediation exercise, in the Quaker sense, is of limited duration, relates to some or all aspects of a specific dispute, involves dealing with responsible officials of governments, liberation movements, or similar entities, and comprises such processes as listening to leaders, the transmission of messages, the reduction or removal of misunderstandings and misperceptions, and sometimes the provision of a suitable venue in which adversaries can meet face-to-face. The Quaker mediation process is thus akin to what the experts call 'good offices'. On those occasions when Friends propose terms of settlement, it is almost always what I have called 'advocacy' (e.g. Korea in 1952) rather than what the experts call 'mediation' since it arises from Quaker initiative rather than at the request or with the express consent of all the parties.

An interesting but abortive effort at mediation (in the Quaker sense) was made by Jack Catchpool in 1918. Catchpool, in Russia for the Friends War Victims Relief Committee, was troubled by the hostage-taking by the two sides in the Civil War. After discussing the matter with G. V. Chicherin, the Bolshevik Commissar for Foreign Affairs, Catchpool agreed to make contact with the White Russian forces under Admiral A. V. Kolchak in the hope that both sides would undertake to end hostage-taking and would exchange an agreed number of hostages as a first step. Trotsky (Commissar of War) signed a paper to the effect that the Bolsheviks would give up hostage-taking if Kolchak's multinational forces would do the same. Catchpool set off by special train for the three-day journey to the front at Kuznetsk. From there, he proceeded on horse-back, wearing a Red Cross brassard, to the White Russian side of the front near Simbirsk (later called Ulyanovsk). He now needed to reach Kolchak's base at Ufa, for which he obtained a permit from the local governor, N. D. Avksentiev. He found Avksen-

*The mediator may be a named individual or even an international agency.

tiev very cooperative, and was able to interview a dozen women hostages whom it was proposed should be part of the first exchange. Avksentiev also arranged for horses and provisions for the return journey. During the night, however, Catchpool was arrested and told that he would be court-martialed for travelling with forged papers and being a Bolshevik spy. During the rest of the night, Catchpool 'dozed, prayed, and felt a new confidence . . . ' The court-martial the next morning took place in a railway wagon. To begin with, it was a very disagreeable affair, the prosecuting general demanding the death penalty. In the middle of the proceedings, however, Avksentiev entered the wagon and confirmed that Catchpool's papers were in order. Catchpool was sent under armed guard in a cattle truck to Siberia, from where he made his own way to Samara (later called Kuybyshev) and thence to the Quaker team at Buzuluk, a journey of several weeks. Jack Catchpool's mediation effort had not been successful.[200]

I have referred earlier to the Lavon affair and the Cairo trials in 1954–5. The ordinary Israeli people, knowing as little about the true facts as did the Quakers, were outraged by Egyptian actions, and pressure mounted that Egypt should be 'punished'. This led to a massive military raid on the Gaza Strip on 28 February 1955 in which 38 Arabs were killed, ostensibly in retaliation for Palestinian guerrilla attacks.[201]

The following April, Elmore Jackson (director of the Quaker office at the UN in New York) met the Egyptian ambassador in Washington, Dr. Ahmed Hussein, and on 15 July, Jackson and I, together with two AFSC colleagues (Lewis Hoskins and Colin Bell) had a meeting with the Egyptian Foreign Minister, Mahmoud Fawzi. As a result of these two meetings, and after consultation with UN, US, and Israeli officials, it was decided that Jackson would undertake a peace mission to the Middle East.[202]

Again, as over the Cairo trial, we acted in ignorance of some crucial facts. When Friends undertake mediation, we always preserve strict confidentiality: if others are mediating, we must assume that they are operating under similar restraints of confidentiality. We do not know whether Jackson's 1955 mission coincided with other non-governmental initiatives. What we *do* know now, but I did not know at the time, is that the previous November, Britain and the United States had reached a top secret agreement to cooperate in an initiative for a comprehensive settlement in the Middle East: this project was known as Operation Alpha.[203]

Jackson went first to Jordan for discussions about relief matters, and thence to Israel, where his most important conversation was with David Ben-Gurion, then Minister of Defence and later in the year Prime Minister. Towards the end of the conversation, Ben-Gurion raised the possibility of a face-to-face meeting with Nasser, the Egyptian Prime Minister. 'Nasser is a decent fellow [Jackson reported Ben-Gurion as saying] who has the interests of his people genuinely at heart.'[204]

From Ben-Gurion's point of view, a direct meeting with Nasser would erode the Arab refusal to recognize the legitimacy of Israel's existence. This was precisely the difficulty from Nasser's point of view, for it would mean defying an agreed Arab stance.[205] No Quaker could dismiss a proposal for a direct meeting of adversaries, however, for surely a well-timed direct meeting might lead to a removal of some misunderstandings and thus to an easing of tensions.

When Jackson reached Cairo, he found that his first meeting with Nasser had been set for 26 August. Jackson could not have foreseen that this was the very day chosen by John Foster Dulles, the US Secretary of State, for a major speech in New York based on Operation Alpha, and that the US ambassador in Cairo had handed Nasser a copy of Dulles's speech at 6 p.m. that evening. According to the ambassador's report to Washington (only recently declassified), Nasser had seemed 'somewhat confused' by the speech and 'did not understand the significance of some passages.' At 7.45 pm that same evening, Jackson saw Nasser, who was undoubtedly in a bemused frame of mind. Nasser did, however, tell Jackson about informal talks between Egyptian and Israeli diplomats in Paris, but that these had been broken off after the Gaza raid in February.[206]

Jackson returned to Israel via Cyprus, only to find it necessary to scale down his tactics from advocating a direct meeting between Egyptian and Israeli politicians and instead to try and stop an impending Israeli attack on Khan Yunis in the Gaza Strip. Jackson reported to the Israelis on his discussions with Nasser and the fact that the Paris talks had been called off because of the Israeli attack on Gaza in February. Another attack, even if provoked by Palestinian incursions, would put an end to all hopes of a direct meeting with Nasser. Later that evening, an Israeli official came to Jackson's hotel to say that Ben-Gurion's military assistant had been sent south to call off the Khan Yunis raid. Public pressure for some kind of retaliatory action was mounting, however, and the Israeli chief of staff, Moshe Dayan, threatened to resign if the raid were not reinstated. During the course of the day, six UN observers were detained by the Israeli authorities in Beersheba, and this led General Burns (head of the UN observer mission) to conclude that 'some military action was in preparation, and the Israelis did not want our observers to see anything of it.' Burns was, indeed, right, for the decision to cancel the Israeli operation had been reversed. The raid took place during the night of 31 August, leading to the deaths of 36 Arabs.[207] Nasser was shocked that this should have happened at a time when he was considering the renewal of direct talks with Israel. Three weeks later, Nasser concluded an agreement for the supply of arms from Czechoslovakia, leading to the cancellation of Anglo-American financing for the Aswan High Dam, Egypt's nationalization of the Suez Canal Co., and the Suez war.[208]

Much of the crucial information on these events was not available to us at the time: what is difficult to decide nearly four decades later is whether, if we had had more information, Friends would have acted differently.

Another Quaker mediation effort regarding the Israel-Arab conflict took place in 1973. On 27 December 1972, I was approached by an Egyptian friend with proposals for direct talks between Egypt and Israel for a peace settlement very much along the lines of the treaty actually concluded in 1979. I asked my friend in what capacity I was being approached: as a student of UN procedures, as chair of the Division of International Affairs of the British Council of Churches, or as a Quaker friend of many years standing. My friend said that the auspices were immaterial from his point of view: he was soliciting my help, and it was up to me to decide what hat to wear. After consulting Quaker colleagues in London, Philadelphia, and the Middle East, it was the united view that this was a job for the Quakers.

One of the difficult questions Friends had to resolve before undertaking such a mediation mission was whether a bilateral settlement between Egypt and Israel would harm Israel's other Arab neighbours or the Palestinians. After much consultation and heart-searching, we came to the conclusion that, on balance, peace between Israel and Egypt could not harm and might marginally advance Palestinian and other Arab interests. Accordingly, Paul Johnson and I agreed to take the Egyptian ideas to Israel for informal discussion with friends in the Foreign Ministry. In addition to the Egyptian suggestions for a bilateral settlement with Israel, we added a Quaker prologue: direct talks between the two sides without preconditions, a moratorium on such future public statements by either party as might make a settlement more difficult to achieve, and an understanding by both parties that positions previously adopted should not be a barrier to the possibility of agreements of substance. With the help of the Bishop of London (Robert Stopford) and the Anglican Archbishop in Jerusalem (George Appleton), it was possible to get a message to a senior Israeli, and the response was sufficiently positive for us to decide to make the trip, and so we arrived at the East Jerusalem YMCA on 28 January 1973.[209]

Our initial reception at the Foreign Ministry the next day, Monday, was initially rather frosty and sceptical, our exposition being interrupted by rude comments on Egyptian personalities and policies. But as the discussion proceeded, the atmosphere lightened, and eventually it was agreed that Paul and I and one of the Israelis would prepare a written account of the Egyptian ideas and a summary of our discussion at Israel's Foreign Office. We were promised a response the following day, Tuesday.

In fact, we had to wait until Friday for Israel's answer, and the atmosphere at the Foreign Ministry was very different from what it had been earlier in the week. Instead of having to endure numerous security checks, we were greeted on the road outside by one of our Israeli friends and conducted directly to a comfortable office. As we were entering the building, the Israeli commented that I was wearing a red tie: did this have political significance? No, I said, but I was in a cheerful mood and it seemed the sort of day for a red tie. Ah, said the Israeli, but it was slightly right of centre: surely that meant something? (Actually, although it was right of centre from his point of view, it was left of centre from mine!)

When we were settled inside, we were told that the message brought by the Quakers had been considered at the highest level of the Israeli Government. Israel was ready for direct talks with Egypt at any place and at any level, without prior assurances or conditions of substance: such talks would necessarily have to be secret. The message brought by the Quakers did not correspond in all respects with Egypt's public posture: which was the true Egyptian position? Meaningful talks would not be possible unless the Israeli side could be assured that the Egyptian side was acting with the full authority of President Sadat. (My Egyptian friend had made it clear in London that we were not to say that the initiative had Sadat's approval.) Our Israeli friends stressed that intermediaries offering good offices might bring about direct contacts between the parties, but should not themselves propose substantive solutions. Israel understood Sadat's difficulties, but had Sadat fully grasped the military realities?

One of the Israelis said that Israel had had good relations with the Quakers in the past. Unfortunately, we lived in a cruel and harsh world, but his own instincts were simple and friendly. Indeed, he thought he would be very happy in the Society of Friends. Israel hoped that the Quakers would continue to keep in touch with both sides. Perhaps the next step would be for a direct Israeli-Egyptian meeting to take place privately in Sydney Bailey's home in London. The only people who knew of the Quaker visit were the Prime Minister (Golda Meir), the Foreign Minister (Abba Eban), the two diplomats with whom we had been in contact, and one official Israeli expert on Arab affairs whose name we were given. The Israeli ambassador in London (Michael Comay) would be informed. While direct talks might not be possible now, the situation might improve, and in a few months time Egypt might be ready to talk on terms acceptable to Israel. The Quaker initiative had been a positive one and its importance would become apparent in due course.

On 20 February, I reported on the conversations in Jerusalem to Hafez Ismail, Sadat's advisor on national security. Quaker peace efforts continued in the Middle East, in London, and at the UN. My wife and I were able to welcome Egyptian and Israeli officials to our home in London, but never simultaneously. In October, the fourth Arab-Israeli war took place. In 1977, Sadat made his historic visit to Jerusalem, Egypt and Israel met at Camp David the following year under President Carter's sponsorship, and a bilateral peace treaty was signed in 1979.

As far as Friends were concerned, we had to ask ourselves whether the peace mission in 1973 had been a right use of limited resources. At the time, there was nothing to show, either positive or negative, but a pamphlet published ten years later by Mordechai Gazit, who was the head of Golda Meir's office at the time, makes it clear that Meir made a 'fundamental change' in policy, a 'far-reaching concession', less than a month after our visit. 'She authorized [Israeli ambassador Yitzhak] Rabin to inform Kissinger that Israel was willing to adopt the idea of 'security in exchange for sovereignty'—or, to simplify, land-for-peace.[210] One might conclude from this that the outcome of our effort was positive, but for the fact that Meir's concession disappeared in the morass of international diplomacy. Meir does not mention the concession in her autobiography. Yitzhak Rabin, in a single sentence in his memoirs, mentions the idea but implies that it originated with Kissinger rather than with Meir, and that Meir agreed with Kissinger only conditionally. Neither Kissinger nor Sadat mention Meir's concession in their memoirs.

Quaker advocacy, reconciliation, and mediation should be seen as complementary: sometimes one process is needed, sometimes another. Indeed, we often have to send exploratory missions to find out which function would be more timely. It would be regrettable were we ever to think of one process as more valuable than the others.

SOME PROCESSES AND PREDICAMENTS OF QUAKER PEACE-MAKING
(i) Concerns, assets, and liabilities.
In this concluding section, I would like to review some of the processes and predicaments of Quaker peace-making. I have drawn on the few published studies of Quaker reconciliation and mediation,[211] on what I have been told orally from colleagues, and on my own experience. As indicated earlier, I can refer only obliquely to recent and current efforts.

It hardly needs saying that the motive of Quaker peace-making is love: love of God and love of neighbour, love of all of God's children and their artefacts of utility or beauty, love of the natural environment.

The origins of particular peace-making operations during the past half century have varied. In the case of the Quaker representatives commuting between the two parts of divided Berlin and the two German states in the 1960s, the initiative came from local Friends. The concern for mediation regarding Southern Rhodesia (now Zimbabwe) was laid on Friends by the British Council of Churches at a time when I chaired its Division of International Affairs. Elmore Jackson's mission to the Middle East in 1955, and the mission to the same area which Paul Johnson and I undertook in 1973, were at the request of one of the parties, with the agreement of the other. In the case of the mission to India and Pakistan in 1966, the Nigeria-Biafra mediation in 1967–69, and the reconciliation and mediation efforts in Sri Lanka in recent years, the concerns originated with two or three Friends and were supported by the relevant Quaker committees. The conciliation work regarding the South Tyrol in 1966 was initiated by Joseph Pickvance after he had asked himself three questions: why had efforts to avert the second world war failed? could conflicts be resolved by the application of academic disciplines? and were the teachings of George Fox still valid today? Pickvance felt he had to test these ideas and so, casting about for a suitable conflict to try them on, 'one not too large nor too distant', he settled on the problem of the South Tyrol (or Alto Adige, as Italians call the region).[212]

But however the concerns have originated, it has almost always been the case that peace-making has been facilitated by previous humanitarian work on one or both sides of the conflict, or by previous Quaker work with diplomats. When Elmore Jackson was in Egypt in 1955, Nasser recalled appreciatively the work of the AFSC for Palestinian refugees in the Gaza Strip and his own recollections of Quaker help when he was beleaguered in the Faluja area in the Negev in 1949. Roland Warren's work in Berlin was made easier by the fact that officials on both sides of the Wall recalled Quaker feeding programmes after the first world war. The 1966 mission to India and Pakistan encountered appreciation on both sides for Quaker humanitarian work. Landrum Bolling reports that when he was working on Middle East issues after the 1967 war, 'One of the advantages we had was finding alumni of Quaker-run international meetings everywhere we went.' In the case of the Nigeria-Biafra mediation, Quaker mediators were in touch with 78 persons all told, of whom 35 had previously participated in Quaker programmes. The difficult mediation effort in Southern Rhodesia was helped by the fact that a senior official of the Smith régime had participated in the Quaker conference for diplomats in 1955 and had subsequently been a member of our London Diplomats Group. Quaker reconciliation in Northern Ireland was a natural outgrowth of the humanitarian work of local Friends.[213]

Those of us who engage in peace-making have no axe to grind other than a wish to help the parties to patch up their quarrel. Mike Yarrow, in his pioneering study of Quaker conciliation to which I referred earlier, notes: 'Quakers have no arms to sell, no ambition to buy oil . . . [they] make the most of their lack of political power.' So far as I know, no group of Friends has ever corporately supported a war, so that Friends have no enemies. We can disregard protocol, be flexible about procedure, commend unilateral gestures or unconventional remedies.

Moreover, we can establish relations with entities like liberation movements with which governments and international agencies may be reluctant to deal.* Our Berlin-based representatives had contacts with the German Democratic Republic long before the GDR was generally recognized, and Mike Yarrow reported that this was appreciated by US officials. In the Nigeria-Biafra case, Quakers made frequent contact with the breakaway area, and British and US Friends have been in constant touch with the Palestine Liberation Organization about Middle Eastern matters: one senior British official accepted my invitation to meet a PLO representative at William Penn House when formal and official contacts were not allowed. Quaker mediators can stick with a problem through thick and thin, whereas ordinary diplomats may be transferred to other posts or be instructed to soft-pedal mediation for extraneous political reasons. It was to avoid the difficulties encountered by ordinary diplomats that Mike Yarrow stressed the importance of continuity of Quaker personnel.[214]

Needless to say, we operate without diplomatic immunity and privileges. When Elmore Jackson was shuttling between Israel and Egypt in 1955, he had to travel via a third country, Cyprus. By the time of his third Tel Aviv-Cairo trip by way of Cyprus, 'the British officers were . . . aware that something unusual was afoot. I was first separated out from the others . . . , then interrogated at some length . . . It was only after all the others had emplaned and the plane's engines started that I was permitted to board.' On the next trip, Jackson broke his journey in Athens. The Berlin-based representatives got to know the border guards quite well. 'A first rule [wrote Mike Yarrow] was that they would never violate the censorship, customs or currency rules.' Requests to do favours for friends by sneaking forbidden material across the frontier were invariably declined: the Quaker workers would open their briefcases and show the frontier guards everything they had.[215]

Quaker peace-makers do not take sensitive material across frontiers, including sealed letters and documents, tapes, unexposed film, and written or other material which it is forbidden to export. Special care is needed about the names of Quaker contacts in areas with oppressive régimes. In 1970, a Quaker representative visited Czechoslovakia and,

---

*Count Bernadotte, the UN mediator in the Middle East in 1948, never made contact with the former Grand Mufti of Jerusalem, who was one of the main Palestinian leaders, and ambassador Gunnar Jarring, who exercised good offices in the Middle East for the UN from 1967 to 1991, tells me that he was never in touch with the Palestine Liberation Organization.

as was the normal custom, he was stopped at the border post when leaving to have his luggage examined. This contained a list of dissidents and other Quaker contacts. He was taken to Brno for interrogation and released after two days. This was not the end of the affair, however, for some time later, an article appeared in a Czechoslovak newspaper alleging that Quaker activities had 'the character of ideological diversion' and served the intelligence services of Czechoslovakia's enemies. The Friends Service Council naturally denied the charges: Quakers were not the servants of any government, maintained FSC, but were concerned only to promote peace and international understanding. We do not know what happened to our contacts in Czechoslovakia: the Friend concerned was no longer able to fulfil the tasks of Quaker representative and so moved to other employment.[216]

In some parts of the world, taxi-drivers report to the authorities on overheard conversations, and hotel rooms may be bugged. When Walter Martin and Trevor Jepson were engaged in mediation regarding Southern Rhodesia (now Zimbabwe) and were in Salisbury (Harare), they were told by one official that the modest hotel in which they were staying was unsuitable for Quakers as it was a favourite haunt of prostitutes and drug-pushers, and another contact warned them that the rooms were bugged. During the Lancaster House conference on Southern Rhodesia/Zimbabwe in 1979, it was widely believed by the Patriotic Front delegates that the British authorities had placed listening devices in their hotel rooms. I was several times warned by friends that the rooms in my favourite hotel in the Middle East were bugged. Even when talking with trusted Quaker colleagues, it was sometimes necessary to take precautions to protect other people, such as to discuss sensitive matters in the open air or in the homes of uncontroversial friends or, if conversations in hotel rooms were unavoidable, to put on a radio or run the taps so as to garble the sound. On one occasion, a bugging device was found on Quaker premises, and on another occasion, sensitive files were tampered with and some items removed from a filing cabinet at Friends House, presumably by agents of a foreign power. During the Nazi times, if a known Gestapo agent entered a Quaker meeting in Germany, the doorkeeper would signal to the clerk, and the clerk would then move the minute book: every Friend knew what this signal meant. It does not come naturally to Friends to act in this way, but sometimes what we have to discuss about peace-making can put other people at risk.

Care has had to be taken when applying for foreign visas: we should neither economize with the truth nor disclose too much sensitive information to lower-level officials. When Sue and Steve Williams (Americans) went to Belfast to engage in reconciliation and mediation for QPS, British officials advised them to apply for visas as missionaries. The fact of having a valid visa does not guarantee that one will be able to enter the country concerned. In June 1976, I was on Quaker business in the Middle East with a valid passport and visas obtained in London for all the countries I wished to visit. When travelling from one Arab country to another, I was taken off the bus and refused entry, though my visa to enter the country concerned was in order. The military officer at the border post never explained to me the reason for the decision, and all my persuasive powers were unavailable. I had no option but to renounce that part of the journey.

Our sympathies are for *all* the people involved in conflict, not for one side or the other. Adam Curle insists that the first task of the peacemaker is to befriend harassed leaders, to listen to their grievances and fears and aspirations. When Roland Warren was in Berlin in the 1960s, he had to make it clear by words and actions that he was not a missionary, a journalist, a pro-Communist American, or a CIA agent. Warren made it a practice never to say anything or agree to anything on one side of the Berlin Wall that he was not prepared to say or defend on the other side.[217]

The Quaker peace-maker does not take sides. During the Suez war of 1956, a US warship evacuating civilians from Alexandria got in the way of British naval operations, so the British admiral asked his US counterpart to move. The US admiral refused but cabled Washington, 'Whose side am I on?'[218] Friends are on the side of peace and justice.

The fact is that all the parties to any dispute or conflict are *victims* of past mistakes. Take the case of Israeli Jews and Palestinian Arabs. The Jews, dispersed throughout the world after their defeat by the Romans in the first two centuries of the Christian era, dreamed of returning one day to the Holy Land. During Passover each year, Jews prayed, 'Next year in Jerusalem'. This was not an expectation that the hope of return would actually be fulfilled during the following twelve months, but an assertion that the dream would one day become a reality for the Jewish people. Then, as oppression of Jews increased in Europe during the nineteenth century, a religious dream became a political goal in the

Zionist movement.* This led in 1917 to the Balfour Declaration pledging British support for 'a national home for the Jewish people' in Palestine, with the proviso that the civil and religious rights of the non-Jewish communities would not be prejudiced. The Nazi policy of persecution and then extermination gave a new impetus to the idea of a place of refuge in Palestine for those Jews unable or unwilling to be assimilated in their countries of residence and, after Britain had referred the Palestine question to the United Nations in 1947 and the UN had decided on partition, a Jewish state rather than simply a homeland for the Jewish people was declared in 1948 but, on the insistence of David Ben-Gurion, a state without defined frontiers. In a number of Israeli-Arab wars, Israel has extended its rule to include the whole of Palestine, so that Palestinian Arabs now live in exile or under foreign occupation.

How does all this look from the point of view of the Palestinian Arabs? Over the centuries, the Arabs had been under the control of a series of non-Arab rulers, culminating in the Ottoman Turks in the sixteenth century. In 1916, Britain and France concluded an agreement whereby certain designated areas under Ottoman rule were to become independent under Arab suzerainty and that, after consultation with the Allies and representatives of Sherif Husayn of Mecca, Palestine was to be under international administration. Husayn and other Arab chiefs were not consulted or informed about this agreement between two European powers at the time it was reached. It was in the expectation of Arab rule over the former Ottoman territories that Husayn was induced to take part in the Arab Revolt against Turkish rule. Palestine and Jordan (then Transjordan) were placed under League of Nations mandate in 1922. Jordan became independent in 1946, Sherif Husayn's great-grandson Hussein now being king. Tension between Jews and Arabs in Palestine made the country increasingly ungovernable, and in 1947 Britain referred the problem to the United Nations. The UN decided to partition the country into Jewish and Arab states, with an international enclave in the Jerusalem-Bethlehem area. The Arabs, knowing that there were then twice as many Arabs as Jews in Palestine, and believing that the UN decision was contrary to the

---

*My great-uncle, David Zvi Farbstein, organized the first Zionist Congress in Basel for Theodor Herzl in 1897. My mother was Jewish so that, according to Jewish law, I was a Jew until I became a Quaker. It is, perhaps, not surprising that my Arab friends sometimes wonder if I am a secret Zionist or that my Jewish friends sometimes wonder if I am a self-hating Jew.[219]

promises made to them during the first world war and that they were being made to suffer because Europeans had ill-treated Jews, went to war to defeat the UN plan. They finished up with less of Palestine than if they had accepted the UN plan in the first place, and lost the rest of the country in 1967 as a result of a war provoked by President Nasser of Egypt but started by Israel.

It seems to me that both Israeli Jews and Palestinian Arabs have inherited their present unhappy situations from their predecessors—though both have compounded past mistakes with mistakes of omission and commission of their own. If we look closely at every conflict, we find that there is a sense in which *all* the parties are in that sense victims. In the case of most refractory conflicts, both parties have long memories. An Arab friend of mine, when asked what was the origin of the Arab-Israeli conflict, spent the first twenty minutes talking about Abraham. Both communities in Northern Ireland date their conflict from the seventeenth century, if not earlier. This syndrome has been called the Tyranny of the Dead.

Friends are not indifferent to questions of right and wrong, but if we are to help the parties to reach agreement, our approach has to be non-judgmental and fair-minded. Impartiality is an elusive concept, however. One cannot be impartial when faced with gross injustice or aggression, but one *can* try to be fair. Adam Curle comments that the mediator has to be 'constantly alert lest an unguarded word give any suggestion of favouritism', and Walter Martin insisted that the reconciler needs an ability 'to view things objectively.' Mike Yarrow considered that one reason for the relative success of the mission to India and Pakistan in 1966 was the team's willingness to assess fairly the pros and cons of each side's position. Elmore Jackson stressed that mediators can help only if they have gained the trust of the parties.[220]

We need to remember that Friends are only a small part of the total picture and that we may not know what other peace-makers are doing. I noted earlier that when Elmore Jackson made his trip to the Middle East in 1955, he was uninformed about the full content of Operation Alpha, the UK-US plan for a comprehensive Middle East settlement, or that Dulles would publicize the main elements of the plan in New York on the very day that Jackson had his first meeting with Nasser. Mike Yarrow noted that in the cases studied in his book on Quaker conciliation, and especially regarding Nigeria-Biafra, 'the Quaker effort was necessarily subordinate and ancillary to conciliation or negotiation by official mediators.' It was only after the mediation effort in Nigeria-Biafra had been under way for some time that Friends learned of parallel initiatives by other church agencies—though some of these other efforts seem to have been rebuffed. At a later stage, Quaker intermediaries found that their message-carrying between the two sides was only one of several channels being used.[221]

From my time at an Anglican school, I recall two prayers relating to peace. One comes in Matins and Evensong, after the congregation has recited the Lord's Prayer. The Priest then prays, 'Give peace in our time, O Lord', to which the congregation responds (I fear unconvincingly, at my school), 'Because there is none other that fighteth for us, but only thou, O God.' The other prayer comes towards the end of the Communion service: 'The peace of God, which passeth all understanding . . .'

The Quaker mediator who wants to help towards the first kind of peace, outer peace, needs to be imbued with the second kind, inner peace. Horace Alexander put it like this: 'No one is likely to be able to influence the actions of statesmen unless he has first learnt to bring peace in his own home and his own heart . . . Or let us say . . . that those who hope to bring peace among the nations must always be striving to remove the seeds of war from their own lives.' Mike Yarrow quoted from a pamphlet in German by Margarethe Lachmund in which she stressed the need for inner peace, but insisted that this inner peace *must* lead to action.[222] Pacifism is not passivism: it is a fruit of love, a source of encouragement in the face of disappointment, of tranquillity in situations of turmoil, of patience in periods of tedium, of courage in times of danger.

Not all Friends have the opportunity to exercise what Paul of Tarsus called 'the ministry of reconciliation'[223] regarding big international conflicts, but Quaker agencies *can* provide dependable administrative support and proper funding to those who *do* have that vocation. In my experience, Quaker mediators operate on a modest scale, and they should be as free as possible from financial anxiety. They deserve, but in the past have not always had, efficient administrative back-up from headquarters. Mike Yarrow reported that the Berlin-based representatives in the 1960s occasionally encountered 'frustrating delays' from the Philadelphia office, and that in the Nigeria-Biafra case, staff support from London and Philadelphia was sometimes lacking: 'an inordinate amount of time' was spent by the Quaker mediators over such humdrum matters as obtaining visas, reserving flights, changing currency, and so on. 'The whole operation was begun and continued on an ad hoc basis, which provided flexibility but lacked continuity and close attention.' Problems in the field are inevitable in this kind of work because opportunities and setbacks are unpredictable. It is to be hoped that the new unit in Quaker Peace and Service which supports our overseas mediation efforts will ensure that administrative under-pinning from London is as dependable as circumstances (and finances) permit.[224]

Quaker peace-makers are non-responsible—which is not to say that we should be irresponsible. All mediators are to some degree responsible for the consequences of their actions, whether these consequences are good or ill, but governmental and inter-governmental mediators may be publicly called to account if they make mistakes and can be reproved, demoted, or fired: the worst that can happen to Quaker mediators who blunder is that they will not be asked by the parties or by Quaker agencies to mediate again. It is an actual *advantage* for a non-official mediator that he or she may be disavowed by the parties at any time.[225]

An undoubted asset for Quaker mediators is the existence of Quaker Houses in New York, Geneva, and Belfast, William Penn House in London, and other similar Quaker centres, where officials can meet privately, informally, and in an atmosphere free of tension. Friends often have to meet officials in offices or in such places as the UN buildings in New York and Geneva. When I was a Quaker representative at the UN in the 1950s, I made it a practice to go to the UN delegates' lounge as often as I could from about 12.30 pm, when the morning sessions began to adjourn, until about 3 pm, when the afternoon sessions were supposed to convene. During the lunch-break, it was possible to have dozens of conversations on matters of Quakerly concern. But these conversations had obvious limitations. They were highly visible, sometimes hurried, it was impossible to avoid the importuning of the media or the noisy announcements on the public address system, they were occasionally overheard, and we could not entirely escape from the climate of confrontation that then characterized the UN. Quaker House, by contrast, was simply our home—informal, away from the glare of publicity. Most diplomats (though perhaps not all) found it easy at Quaker House to relax, to shed their official roles, to become human beings facing difficulty and perplexity. Quaker centres were

Metropolitan Nikodim of the Russian Orthodox Church with a group of Friends at William Penn House, 1967.

invaluable during the conferences on Southern Rhodesia, in Geneva in 1976 and in London in 1979.[226]

One danger of all Quaker peace-making is that of spiritual arrogance. We are motivated by deeply-held concern, but concern sometimes slides into conceit. We know from our own Quaker experience how difficult it can be to discover corporately the will of God on complex issues (taxation for military purposes, for example, or participation in ecumenical activities). Secular bodies like governments and liberation movements are not trying to seek the will of God but are simply weighing the advantages and disadvantages of alternative courses of action. We must avoid attitudes of moral superiority towards those we wish to help.

I have quoted earlier Hugh Tinker's comment that the members of the India Conciliation Group were self-appointed and came from the same social class. Mike Yarrow noted that the Quaker Establishment could be criticized as middle-class and élitist, 'a fact only partly corrected by the wisdom of Quaker leaders in the past and present who have recognized the limitation and tried to overcome it.' Some Friends in India were troubled by the attitude of British Friends to the India-Pakistan conflict in 1965, and some Friends in east and central Africa believed that they had not been sufficiently consulted or involved in the early stages of Quaker mediation regarding Southern Rhodesia.[227]

There are times when Quakers of more than one nationality can be more effective peace-makers than Quakers from the same country. The peace-making efforts regarding India-Pakistan, Nigeria-Biafra, and Sri Lanka have been Anglo-American enterprises, and I was glad to be in partnership with an American Friend, Paul Johnson, in the Middle East mission in 1973. American Friends have made outstanding contribution to reconciliation in Northern Ireland. It should be recognized, nevertheless, that the styles of the Quaker agencies in London and Philadelphia sometimes differ. Mike Yarrow considered that Carl Heath's plan for Quaker embassies aroused 'some misgivings' in the United States: London stressed the overt Quaker message of pacifism, while Philadelphia stressed the need to relieve suffering. Writing of the selection of the team for the India-Pakistan mission, Yarrow noted that London emphasized as a qualification 'the strength of Quaker background' while Philadelphia put the main stress on 'knowledge and experience in the subcontinent.'[228] In the case of the Southern Rhodesian mediation, there were difficulties because of the different political stands of Philadelphia and London. Philadelphia took a militant position against racist régimes and was unwilling to have direct dealings in Southern Rhodesia with Ian Smith or his colleagues. London, while no less hostile to racism than Philadelphia, took the view that, if the problem were to be solved with a minimum of violence, negotiations with the Smith régime were unavoidable. The result was that the American Friends who took part in the Quaker peace process were not appointed by the AFSC but recruited directly by London. The AFSC representative in Southern Africa, Bill Sutherland, was present during the Geneva conference in 1976 and part of the Lancaster House conference in 1979, but on the whole he acted independently of his Quaker colleagues. Lyle Tatum, a veteran AFSC worker, was in London for much of the Lancaster House conference at the request of the Friends Service Council and was in Salisbury (Harare) the following year for AFSC. Cooperation with British Friends was generally but not invariably satisfactory.

I have referred earlier to the problems that arise when different Quaker agencies, or different parts of the same agency, act in such a way as to undercut the other. This is especially acute when advocacy in print complicates the confidential work of Quaker mediators. Such problems are probably not completely avoidable, but every effort should be made to avoid taking Quaker colleagues by surprise. British Quaker mediators report regularly and confidentially in writing to the general secretary and area secretary of QPS, who inform the clerk of the relevant committee: staff and clerk then decide together how much sensitive information should be shared on a confidential basis with the committee. In the case of the Southern Rhodesian mediation, the only reference in the minutes of the Southern African Working Group to the existence of a Quaker team at the Geneva conference in 1976 was to ask Isabel Taylor to chair a meeting as the regular clerk, Trevor Jepson, was in Geneva.[229]

Oran Young, one of the most perceptive students of the role of intermediaries in international politics, has written that a mediator will not embark on a peace-making mission without first weighing the likely benefits and costs *to the mediator*. Young had in mind such benefits as increased salary, enhanced reputation, and a variety of intangible rewards. Costs include a recurring sense of frustration and the knowledge that unsuccessful mediation may reduce the intermediary's chances of mediating successfully in the future.[230] I do not think that

Young's assessment applies to the Quaker peace-makers I have known. Adam Curle recalls no case in which those engaged in non-official mediation have been paid, other than their out-of-pocket expenses.[231] I have never had my salary increased or reduced as a result of undertaking mediation, nor do I think my reputation has been damaged or enhanced: and if there have been 'intangible rewards', I have been unaware of them. But I admit to having experienced a sense of frustration, caused as much by my own mistakes as by the intransigence of the parties.

Where do we find Quaker mediators to meet the demands made on us, whether initially arising from our own religious concern or as a result of requests from the parties which then sparks off our concern? Sometimes there are full-time Quaker representatives in the field who form the nucleus of a team of about five from whom the members for each particular phase can be chosen. Other members of the team are likely to include staff at headquarters, employees of Quaker charitable trusts, and retired Friends. But those sources will not provide enough Friends to undertake work that is open-ended in time and where continuity of personnel is essential. (The Sri Lankan mediation had continued for nine years when this book went to press.)[232]

I think we must set about recruiting potential Quaker mediators from other sources—Quaker schools, institutions like Woodbrooke and Charney Manor, Quaker academics, social workers, and so on. Training and the sharing of experiences will be possible at the new body called 'Responding to Conflict' based at Woodbrooke or at the Centre for Conflict Resolution at the University of Bradford. We particularly need more women among Quaker mediators. The QPS report on mediation makes it clear that there are places where women are 'culturally not as acceptable as men in the mediating role', but there may be other situations where women are more qualified than men. Our policy should be to 'promote sensitively our testimony to the equality of the sexes' so long as this does not harm the mediating process.[233]

(ii) **The peace process**. Before embarking on a mediation mission, an early opportunity should be sought to consult local Friends (if there are any), especially if Quaker mediation is likely to expose them to difficulties, threats, or dangers. When Friends were contemplating a mission to India and Pakistan after the fighting in 1965, Horace Alexander

stressed in the pages of *The Friend* that 'the way to gain all is to surren-
der all.' He concluded, 'Would that the land of Gandhi might act by
this profound truth.' This led to a pained letter a few weeks later from
Ranjit Chetsingh, a distinguished Indian Friend, expressing sadness
that Friends were prone to 'still their restless minds by seeking easy
avenues for the expression of their troubled feelings and earnest spir-
its.' Work for peace and understanding, he wrote, called for more than
'dramatic missions of well-meaning visitors.' Friends should work
side-by-side *with* Indian peace-lovers, not *for* them.[234]

When Paul Johnson and I were engaged in mediation in the Middle
East, we informed the small Quaker group in Ramallah about our
activities in general terms, but not about the details of every conversation. Ramallah Friends made it clear that this was not work to which
they felt called, but they were consistently supportive of our efforts. In
the case of the Nigeria-Biafra mediation, Friends in East Africa were
informed of the activities of British and American Friends. Less care
seems to have been taken to inform or involve East African Friends
over the mediation regarding Southern Rhodesia (Zimbabwe),
although Ernest Shivutse from East Africa was a member of the
Quaker team during the Geneva Conference in 1976.[235]

I have referred earlier to the desirable spiritual attributes of the
peace-maker, the need for inner peace before we can help the parties to
move towards outward peace. But preparation is also needed at the
secular level: acquiring information about the issues in dispute, about
the characters and foibles of the leaders on the two sides, about other
mediation efforts in train or being planned. Elmore Jackson, although
no stranger to the Middle East, spent four months on what he called
'my homework on the basic issues' before visiting the region in 1955.
Other Quaker mediators have stressed the importance of homework:
Roland Warren, Joseph Pickvance, Adam Curle, Landrum Bolling.
Horace Alexander wrote that the first lesson from Gandhi's peace-
making was the need for long and hard training, to immerse oneself in
the language and culture of an area before expecting to help in the
peace process. Adam Curle notes that non-official mediators have no
established sources of intelligence information, and Landrum Bolling
warns that non-official mediators, not knowing what is going on at the
governmental level, may easily become 'meddlers'.[236] On one occasion, I had to turn down a proposal for a mediating mission because
there was insufficient time for 'homework' before the mission had to

begin. It was a hard decision to take, as lives were at stake, and it was not easy to explain my decision to those who had requested help.

'Homework' includes seeking information and views from a wide range of people who know about the conflict—Quaker colleagues, academics, diplomats, international officials. I have made a practice of consulting as widely as possible before a trip, and reporting discreetly to trusted friends on my return; but while engaged on a peace mission, I steer clear of British diplomatic posts. When Paul Johnson and I were in Israel in 1973, we made no contact with the US or British embassies or consular posts. That seems to have been the general practice of Quaker mediators.[237] An exception to this practice was Elmore Jackson, who reported regularly to US diplomats in the course of his 1955 mission, and he attended two meetings of the US National Security Council on his return.[238] On more than one occasion, governments have offered to defray the expenses of Quaker mediation, but I believe that such offers have always been politely declined.

The peace-maker needs to be familiar with the jargon about the conflict. In Northern Ireland, for example, 'union' means union between Northern Ireland and Great Britain, 'unity' means union between Northern Ireland and the Irish Republic—though in the South and in international organizations, the country we call the Republic of Ireland is known simply as Ireland. We have to learn the nuances between Protestant, unionist, and loyalist, and between Catholic, nationalist, and republican. It is usually better to say 'para-military' rather than 'terrorist'.

In the Middle East, it is useful to know the substance of major UN resolutions: 181 (partition of Palestine), 194 (rights of refugees), 242 (principles for a Middle East settlement). Syria did not accept resolution 242 when it was passed in 1967, but seven years later Syria accepted resolution 338 re-affirming resolution 242, so in Damascus, one always says 'resolutions 242 *and* 338.' Israelis call the war between the Arabs and Israel in 1973 'the Yom Kippur War', Arabs (especially if they are Muslims) call it 'the Rămadăn War': if in doubt, call it 'the 1973 war'. The Palestinian territories captured by Israel in 1967 are called by Israel 'the administered territories', by Arabs 'the occupied territories': it is sometimes best simply to call them 'the territories'. There may be occasions when it is useful to know that Golda Meir started life as Golda Myerson or that Yasser Arafat's original name was Abu Ammar. What the Iranians call the Persian Gulf and Arabs call the Arab Gulf can be called simply 'the Gulf'. (In one Quaker-sponsored conference on peace in the Middle East, we had to call this area 'the Eastern sub-region of the Middle East'.) In his final annual report as UN Secretary-General in 1991, Pérez de Cuéllar called the former Soviet Union 'the northern Eurasian land mass'.[239] Such clumsy circumlocutions are sometimes unavoidable.

I have learned by experience and from colleagues a number of tips about outward demeanour for the Quaker peace-maker. We dress simply and appropriately for the occasion, taking account of local climate and customs. It helps, of course, if one is fluent in the local language: if not, we learn a few simple phrases, such as greeting on arrival and farewell on departure. We try to sit comfortably, neither too casual nor too formal. We look intently at the speaker and try to appear interested, even if we have heard it all a hundred times before. We may be offered coffee, tea, fruit juice, or mineral water by a servant who does not speak English: we learn the local words for saying 'thank you' and any gestures for accepting or rejecting a second portion. We try to discover in advance whether, if we are offered food, it is courteous to leave some uneaten food on one's plate at the end of the meal or to eat every last scrap. Before visiting Egypt in 1955, Elmore Jackson made a point of reading Nasser's *Egypt's Liberation*. 'My interest [in one episode] unleashed a wellspring of recollection and reflection . . . It was clear that I had touched deep wells.' Jackson told Nasser that he had been reading the Koran, and Nasser later sent Jackson a book on Islam.[240]

When meeting leaders during a mediation mission, I try to ask a secretary or assistant in advance of the conversation how much time the official has set aside, and I make tentative moves to leave a few minutes before zero hour—while being prepared to stay longer if that is what the host clearly wishes. I normally do not take notes during a conversation but reconstruct the main points in writing later with the help of my Quaker colleague. My only exception to this practice is when the speaker says something crucially important, and especially if it differs in some degree from public policy. In that event, I ask permission to write it down, and read it back to make sure that I have correctly understood and have an accurate record. If the mediator has contacts on the other side, he or she should try to find an early opportunity of making this known.[241] If necessary, ask whether what you are being told is for your own private information or may be passed on to the other side. Never belittle one side in the presence of the other, whatever your personal views may be: one of your chief tasks is to create trust so that both sides will take risks for peace. I recall with shame an occasion when Friends were engaged in a particularly delicate mediation exercise. At a meeting at William Penn House with the leaders of one of the parties, we made the mistake of denigrating the leader of another party, even suggesting that he was the stooge of a foreign power. That undoubtedly reduced our effectiveness.

Trust has to be built up gradually. Roland Warren made a practice of not placing premature strains on a relationship. 'One might be able to say some things after a relationship of credibility has been firmly established that would be highly inflammatory if said too early in the relationship.'[242]

Quaker mediation teams should ideally consist of two or sometimes three persons for each conversation. A single mediator finds the role too lonely, more than three becomes a delegation, and this makes it difficult to achieve the right degree of informality. Two or three persons can divide up responsibilities, supply missing information, identify flexibilities of position, watch for non-verbal communications, and share in making the humdrum practical arrangements.

When Elmore Jackson went to the Middle East in 1955, he was accompanied during the Egyptian phases by Meado Zaki, who had formerly been Dean of the Cairo School of Social Work and had worked closely with the AFSC team in the Gaza Strip in 1949; but Jackson went alone to his meeting with Nasser and other Egyptian leaders. The general Quaker experience since then has been that it is better to work in pairs or trios. Mike Yarrow found this to be true in all the cases he studied.

> The work alternated between long periods of tedium, discouragement, and confusion and bouts of excitement, exhilaration and tension. Members of a mission could help each other keep a calm perspective . . . Closely tied to this emotional and psychological support was the benefit of more than one mind in analyzing tangled issues, preparing to maximize the brief time of an interview, or figuring out next steps.[243]

There were times during the mediation efforts regarding Southern Rhodesia (Zimbabwe) when crucial decisions had to be taken in difficult circumstances by lone Friends. This was particularly the case regarding hastily-written letters in 1979 from Bishop Muzorewa in Salisbury to the two liberation movements and the Presidents of Zambia and Tanzania. After two of the four letters had been delivered, Walter Martin learned from President Nyerere of Tanzania of a Southern Rhodesian air-raid against Lusaka in Zambia the previous night, and Martin had to decide at short notice and without consultation with colleagues whether to deliver the other two letters. In a very difficult and tense situation, Martin decided that it would do more harm than good to deliver the other two letters, though one of the letters was later transmitted indirectly to the intended recipient.[244]

We have to remember at all times that the Quaker mediators are not normally in physical danger, though Jack Catchpool had a most unpleasant experience of being arrested and charged with espionage while engaged in a peace mission in Russia in 1918, Margaret Barber of the War Victims Relief Committee was arrested by White Russians in Azerbaijan in 1919, Corder Catchpool was arrested in Berlin in 1933 and in Prague in 1938, Elsie Fox Howard was held by the Gestapo in 1935, and Quaker relief workers were detained for a time by the Viet Cong during the Vietnam war. But I know of no cases in which Quaker workers have lost their lives while engaged in peace missions. We should realize, however, that our activities may put others at risk. When Sa'id Hammami first came to London to represent the Palestine Liberation Organization, he was eager to demonstrate his militancy by showing pictures of himself in combat fatigues and carrying a gun. Gradually, over the years, he came to soft-pedal the military option and stress the need for Palestinian Arabs to co-exist with Israeli Jews. He was assassinated in 1978 by agents of the extremist Abu Nidal Palestinian faction a couple of hours after I had visited him in his office in Green Street.*[245] The Scotland Yard detective investigating Hammami's murder told me that there was a box of Quaker peace literature in his office. And there have been other comparable cases of local people with whom Friends were in touch being murdered: in Northern Ireland, Southern Rhodesia, and Sri Lanka.[246]

How should we respond to requests to intercede for or even to provide sanctuary for individuals who are exposed to gross injustice or

---

*According to Patrick Seale, an expert on Arab politics, the Abu Nidal group was also responsible for the grenade attack on the Akropole Hotel in Khartoum on 15 May 1988. This killed a Sudanese waiter, a Sudanese army officer, Chris and Clare Rolfe and their two young children, and Sally Rockett. Chris and Clare Rolfe had worked for Quaker Peace and Service in Somalia; Sally Rockett was an attender at York meeting.

danger? I doubt whether any general answer will fit all the circumstances that are likely to arise, but I have suggested earlier three questions we should ask ourselves in such cases (p.116). Mike Yarrow pointed out that for a mediator to intercede for individuals holds 'grave risks', as it changes an impartial intermediary into an advocate for or against one side, though he suggested that 'discreet inquiries' may sometimes be appropriate. He then posed a series of questions.

What can realistically be accomplished and by what means?
What are others doing?
Will protests from some sources only make matters worse?
What will be the relative value and effectiveness of private versus public appeals?
Can the rapport with the authorities built up over the years bear the weight of direct appeals for justice and clemency, which may imply a challenge to those authorities?[247]

The timing of mediation can be crucial. Many academic writers on the subject suggest that mediation is most likely to succeed when there is a military balance between the parties, so that neither side believes that it can gain more from military threats and acts than from seeking a negotiated solution. There are doubtless cases where that has been true, but my own experience has been that a willingness to negotiate, and to accept the help of a third party, depends primarily on the confidence of political leaders in the united support of their own public opinion. Time and again the Government of Israel has failed to respond positively to proposals for peace because of divisions among the leaders (1971, 1975, 1991). On the other hand, Sadat was able to take risks for peace after the 1973 war because, although Egypt was relatively weak in military terms, Sadat believed that his conciliatory stance had the backing of mainstream opinion in Egypt. The QPS report on mediation stresses the importance of maintaining contact with the parties, over many years if necessary, so that mediation may be offered at the right moment. A decision on timing may ultimately be a religious one, 'a moment of truth, divinely or intuitively revealed, but not amenable to explanation or analysis.'[248]

Governments like to probe informally before proposing formally. An official may be instructed to make an informal and ostensibly personal approach to a foreign government in order to test the water. Here is an example from the recent memoirs of a European head of government.

... I decided to allow Michael to pursue this strategy on a personal basis with British officials in a manner that would not engage my authority or that of the Government, which I did not wish to involve in the preparation of concrete proposals at this stage—unless the course of these soundings evoked a positive response, in which case I would have to address the question of how far along this road the Government would be willing to go.[249]

The help of an intermediary may be sought when the parties do not feel able to put forward proposals for peace but might accept ideas submitted by others. Egyptian ambassador Ahmed Hussein told Elmore Jackson in 1955 that 'it was easier for Egypt to respond to suggestions made by others.' The role of an honest broker is important when the parties are not yet ready for direct contacts. Mike Yarrow reported that in the cases he studied, the long-term goal of the Quaker intermediaries was at all times 'talks under official auspices', and Adam Curle notes that the role of the non-official peace-maker is not to negotiate but to help create favourable conditions for negotiation: mediation 'has to be followed-up by skilled negotiation, usually directly between the protagonists.'[250]

'Most men in handling public affairs', wrote François de Callieres in 1716, 'pay more attention to what they themselves say than what is said to them . . . One of the most necessary qualities in a good negotiator is to be an apt listener.'[251]

The Quaker mediator certainly has to learn to be a good listener. The parties to a conflict nearly always consider that the rest of the world fails to understand their grievances. Moreover, people with grievances (including Quakers) often gain psychological release from being able to articulate them. And, from the point of view of the mediator, it is necessary to listen carefully, not only as a matter of courtesy, but also to identify any nuance in what the speaker is saying which may differ even in minor degree from her or his publicly declared position. It is not necessarily wise to draw attention to any such nuanced statement, but one can tactfully ask the official to repeat or elaborate what has been said. If it becomes clear that one is being given a revised position on some aspect, it may be necessary to ask if this is for the private information of the Quakers or to be conveyed to the other side. A special difficulty arises when an official stresses that he is expressing a personal view and not necessarily that of his government—though he may have been instructed to say that! It was 27 years after his peace mission in 1955 that Elmore Jackson learned that it was fully supported by Nasser.[252]

Almost all those who have written about Quaker mediation stress the art of good listening. 'Being able to listen', Landrum Bolling has written, 'is probably the most important quality an informal diplomat should bring to his task.' 'Listening and asking questions is the least threatening of third-party procedures,' wrote Mike Yarrow. In the case of the India-Pakistan mission in 1966, the team members 'could predict the selection of facts and history that would be given . . . Although eventually totally familiar with these recitals, the team members felt it was necessary to listen, nod their heads dutifully, and occasionally raise some pointed questions.'[253]

Many of the people we have to listen to are congenial to Friends, but there can be times when patient listening does not come easily to us: listening to those who engage in or condone political murder or terrorism, for example, or feed us with false information. But these people may have a story to tell, grievances to relate, disappointments to declare. Quaker mediators do not choose the parties to the conflict but deal with all those *de facto* authorities whose agreement is needed if peace and justice are to be achieved.

Some disputes arise from objective clashes of interest between the parties, but nearly always these objective conflicts of interest are overlaid and exacerbated by misunderstandings about the intentions of the other side. Although the mediator should try to avoid unthinking and rigid cultural stereotyping, there is no getting away from the fact that communities of people tend to develop different ways of thinking. Here is an account of a conversation between a leading Western official and an Asian cleric during the Vietnam war.

It was a very revealing meeting, and also very frustrating . . . It was a wonderful example of what happens when a surgical, cold, highly-trained mind . . . is confronted with a lofty, spiritual unfocused . . . approach to the practical matters of the day . . . [I]t could serve as almost a classical study of the intellectual differences between the West and the East . . . But the stakes were very high, and it was terribly frustrating to see these two people . . . simply incapable of understanding what each other meant.[254]

After the Arab-Israeli war of 1973, the well-known Egyptian

journalist, Mohamed Heikal, interviewed Henry Kissinger. After the conversation was over, Heikal mused on the differences between Arab and Western concepts of truth. Kissinger, he wrote, 'comes from a school which believes that the truth is what we see at this moment, and not what we think or believe as a consequence of what has happened before.' At the Camp David meeting in 1978, President Carter told President Sadat that his stance on one issue was not logical, to which Sadat replied, 'Some things in the Middle East are not logical or reasonable. For Egypt, this is one of them.'[255]

Misperceptions and misreadings can occur about two aspects of the other side, its capabilities and its intentions. Capabilities include objective and tangible elements that can be counted, such as population, gross domestic product, numbers and equipment of the armed forces, and so on. Capabilities also include intangible elements like morale of the people, alertness of officials, the ability to repair damage quickly, the stability of the internal political system, and so on. We know from past experience how widely wrong the assessment of the capabilities of other countries can be—witness the failure of the three invading countries at Suez in 1956 to foresee the ability of the international community to force a military withdrawal, the faulty US assessment of the tangible and intangible capabilities of the Viet Cong in the 1960s, the Soviet miscalculation of the cost of sending troops to Afghanistan in 1979, and Iraq's mistaken estimate of the ability of the United Nations to organize a military coalition to expel Iraqi forces from Kuwait in 1990–91. There is very little that the independent intermediary can do about faulty assessments of *capabilities*.

The assessment of *intentions* is another matter. Intentions can change, witness President Sadat's historic visit to Jerusalem in 1977 and the decision of the Palestine Liberation Organization in 1988 to accept UN Security Council resolution 242 concerning the principles for a Middle East peace settlement more than twenty years after the resolution was passed. Moreover, one way of modifying the intentions of the other side is by your own actions. When President Nasser expelled the UN peace-keeping force and closed the Gulf of Aqaba to Israeli cargoes in 1967, this changed Israel's intentions from a posture of vigilant self-defence to a decision to launch a pre-emptive war. But if one kind of unilateral act can exacerbate tension, another kind can reduce it. The published literature on Quaker peace-making is replete with examples of attempts to bring about a reduction in tension by suggestions of unilateral confidence-building gestures by one or both sides. Roland Warren, who was based in Berlin in the 1960s and commuted between the two sides, has stressed that a mediator should always have in mind 'two or three specific steps that might be taken at no risk to either side, which would tend to reduce tensions and lead to the resolution of other, more important issues.' In the case of the Nigeria-Biafra war, Quaker mediators several times suggested unilateral steps to each side 'such as pauses in bombing, daytime relief flights, and a halt to propaganda.'[256] In trips to the Middle East after the Iraqi invasion of Kuwait in 1990, I had in my briefcase a paper which started with unilateral steps that Iraq and the UN Coalition could take separately or simultaneously to reduce tension and lessen the risks of military action.

The Quaker inclination is to regret the lack of trust between parties in dispute, but in some cases of acute conflict, there are sound reasons for all the parties to distrust the others. 'Instead of appealing for greater trust, I tend to ask the parties if there are any gestures of goodwill . . . to reverse the cycle of fear.'[257] One asks side A, 'can you think of any actions which side B can take without risk which would increase your confidence in the possibility of a peaceful solution?' This usually leads to a torrent of suggestions. When the flood has subsided, one next asks, 'If side B were to make one or more of these gestures, what response could *you* make to increase the *other* side's confidence?' This is often followed by an embarrassed pause, but gradually one is sometimes able to elicit some reciprocal steps. The challenge to the mediator is then to establish a series of unilateral reciprocal steps, coordinated in time. This technique was advocated by UN Secretary-General Dag Hammarskjold after his trip to the Middle East in the spring of 1956. The problem of respect for the 1949 armistice agreements could not be solved by explicit agreements between the parties, he wrote, 'because it is essentially a question of co-ordinated unilateral moves inspired by greater confidence in the possibility of a peaceful development, each of them provoked by and, maybe, provoking similar unilateral moves on the other side.'[258]

Sometimes misunderstanding arises from straightforward factual error. On 15 March 1972, King Hussein of Jordan made an important speech in the course of which he said: 'With the issue of the Balfour Declaration in 1917, the formation of the state of Jordan gained yet a new dimension, in that it made it possible to exclude the land east of the Jordan River . . . from the Zionist schemes of that period.' By some mischance, the translation of the speech from Arabic into Hebrew changed 'east' of the Jordan River to 'west'. On the basis of this mistranslation, Prime Minister Golda Meir of Israel denounced the King's speech in Israel's parliament the following day. She referred to the passage I have quoted, except that she changed 'east bank' (Jordan) to 'west bank' (Israel). King Hussein, she said, was extending his ambitions to 'our country' (Israel) and was crowning himself as king of Jerusalem. I happened to be in the Middle East at the time and, reading both speeches in English translations, noticed the mistake. I was able to draw the matter to the attention of Israeli officials, who courteously expressed appreciation and regret. The damage had been done, however.

All Quaker mediators have encountered the way misperceptions and distortions exacerbate every dispute. The problem arises in part because each side knows that opinion on its own side is divided, but believes that opinion on the other side is monolithic. When political leaders speak in public, they address multiple audiences. What is said to reassure domestic opinion may have the effect of increasing anxiety on the other side. Roland Warren, with experience of divided Germany and divided Korea, has commented how every act by an opponent was explained by a few selected motives which were in keeping with an over-simplified picture of the real state of affairs. 'Measures adopted to protect one side from the unreliability of the opponent encourage counter-measures which increase this alleged unreliability.' Mike Yarrow noted how relations between India and Pakistan were aggravated by 'distortions, delusions and falsifications', so that a prime task of the Quaker mission was to demonstrate to the opposing leaders that their counterparts on the other side 'were also reasonable and well-meaning people, motivated by similar ideas and pressures.' However, this tactic sometimes proved counter-productive, according to Yarrow. When the leaders on one side of the India-Pakistan dispute were told that the leaders on the other side were saying much the same sort of thing as they were saying, this was taken to demonstrate the depravity of the other side for justifying their blatant aggression as self-defence.'[259]

It is because misunderstandings cause such havoc that Quaker mediators find themselves carrying messages from one side to the other, usually oral messages but sometimes in written form. This message-carrying role may be at the express request of one of the parties, or it may seem a constructive task for the Quakers to propose. Elmore Jackson was shown a draft letter from Prime Minister Sharett of Israel which Jackson was to take to Prime Minister Nasser in Cairo; but in the end, Sharett decided not to send the letter but to let Jackson 'handle the crisis in his own way.' I have referred earlier to the letter which Bishop Muzorewa asked Walter Martin to carry to the two liberation front leaders and Presidents Nyerere and Kaunda. The QPS handbook on mediation warns, however, 'never carry sealed messages or secret documents.'[260]

More usually messages are oral, and it is for this reason that we have to take special care that we have understood accurately every nuance of the message we have been asked to convey. When I was in Jerusalem in 1973, one of the Israeli officials suddenly interrupted the exposition of the Egyptian message with the remark that this did not correspond to Egypt's public position. Fortunately, I had with me the notes I had made after talking with my Egyptian friend. The distinction between the message and Egypt's public position, while not of great substantive importance, clearly intrigued the Israeli officials.

Mike Yarrow noted that Quaker message-carrying was particularly important during the Nigeria-Biafra war. Message-carrying, if handled with discretion, is less threatening to the parties and less dangerous to the intermediary than other roles, such as making proposals for settlement. Yet Yarrow pointed out that on one occasion, Friends refused to carry a message from one side to the other on the ground that the errand 'hardly conformed to the role of a neutral mediator.' (General Odd Bull, the chief UN observer in Jerusalem, faced a similar predicament on the first day of the Israeli-Arab war of 1967, when he was asked to transmit a message from Israel to Jordan which he thought contained a threat. It was not the 'normal' practice of the UN to pass on threats from one government to another, but the situation that day was not normal, and Bull transmitted the message.)[261]

If Quaker mediators are asked to propose the terms of settlement (which, in my experience, does not happen very often), can they advocate solutions that are inconsistent with Quaker principles? Personally, I would never *propose* to the parties actions inconsistent with Quaker principles, but consider a situation in which the Quaker mediator is not advocating a particular solution but merely acting as a go-between. I was once asked by a party to a dispute to take a package of proposals to the opposing party. Many of the items in the list were eminently acceptable to Friends: mutual release of prisoners, for example, both sides to terminate attacks on the good faith of the other sides' leaders, and so on. But one item read, 'joint military manoeuvres'. After some hesitation, I decided to transmit the package and, if the chance arose, to make clear the stand of Friends on military forces. This sort of thing is not likely to happen very often, and the message should be carried only after careful thought and consultation by the Friends directly concerned; but I could not assert that it would *never* be right for Friends to transmit such a plan from one side to the other if they believed that to do so would serve the cause of peace and justice.[262]

Related to the question of carrying messages that include ethically dubious elements is whether Friends should mediate between the oppressor and the oppressed. To put the issue like that is , of course, to over-simplify a complex problem. An oppressive régime is likely to perform *some* acts that are good, and an organization of oppressed people is likely to do *some* things that are bad. Many Friends thought that Communism provided an ethical challenge to the West, even though its methods were often sinister.[263] Many Friends have approved the broad aims of some liberation movements but have deplored the fact that some of their members committed atrocities from time to time. In conflicts for which Quaker mediation is desired, righteousness is never all on one side.

In 1953, Friends joined the other Historic Peace Churches and the International Fellowship of Reconciliation in publishing a pamphlet, *Peace is the Will of God*. The content of the pamphlet was unremarkable, a conventional exposition of Christian pacifism. I was very pleased with the title, however. Two years later, the mainstream Churches published a response drafted by Reinhold Niebuhr and Angus Dun, with an even better title, *God wills both Justice and Peace*. Bertram Pickard stressed that religious pacifists never condone or collude with evil.[264]

At the same time, mediators (like marriage guidance counsellors) do not have to reach a judgment on the moral character of the parties. We have to ask a much more difficult question: will an increase in mutual understanding and a reduction in tension be likely, in both the short and long term, to produce a more just outcome than if the conflict is allowed to simmer? When we went on a mediation mission to the Middle East in 1973, we had to ask ourselves whether a bilateral peace between Egypt and Israel would damage the legitimate goals of other Arabs in the region. Rightly or wrongly, we decided that, on balance, it would not.[265]

The Quaker mediator's primary task is not to propose how the problem should be solved but to make it easier for the two sides to communicate. Roland Warren, the Quaker representative in Berlin in the 1960s, held strongly to the view that the Quaker role was to facilitate communication rather than to advocate preconceived solutions.[266] There can be exceptions, of course. Elmore Jackson twice made proposals, once on his own initiative, and once at the request of one of the parties; Roland Warren's successors in Berlin made suggestions from time to time for dealing with humanitarian and sometimes even political issues; the Quaker team in Nigeria-Biafra put forward a number of ideas for easing the tension and on one occasion commended a paper on federalism by a US academic.[267] Quaker advocacy of particular solutions may sometimes be right, but it can easily backfire and undermine the mediating role.

Quaker mediation has to be conducted under terms of strict confidentiality. For it to become known that a party to a dispute is contemplating a peaceful settlement may simply increase the other side's intransigence. Moreover, I have more than once been told by officials that everyone will be astonished at the concessions their side will offer once negotiations begin. Gideon Rafael of Israel made this point to Elmore Jackson in 1955, and the Biafrans made a similar point to the Quakers in 1968.[268]

I have mentioned earlier that when a few of us saw Selwyn Lloyd about a Korean settlement in 1952, he gave us one item of information about British Government policy for our own most confidential information only. Naturally we respected that confidence—which was just as well, as British Government policy on the issue changed six weeks later. Elmore Jackson gave assurances of confidentiality before his Middle East trip in 1955. Sometimes unwanted publicity can damage a mediating effort, as happened on one occasion over Nigeria-Biafra in 1968.[269]

Friends have an instinctive faith in the value of face-to-face meetings between adversaries. There are, I believe, several reasons for this. It is one of the ways we deal with differences of judgment within our own Society, well illustrated by John Woolman's pleading with Quaker slave-owners. When differences arise between ourselves and the secular authorities, we (or at least I) like to deal with officials face-to-face, for I do not find it easy to answer that of God in the other person on the phone or by post. Quaker mediators soon get to like the leaders on the two sides of a conflict and take it for granted that, if only they could meet face-to-face, they would come to like each other. As almost all conflicts are exacerbated by misperceptions, it is believed that these would soon be reduced or eliminated by frank face-to-face talks between leaders.

Elmore Jackson's original hope in 1955 had been to arrange direct talks between Ben-Gurion and Nasser, and he later concluded that he allowed the leaders on the two sides to spend too much time considering this. Roland Warren spent a lot of time in the 1960s promoting the idea of a direct meeting of intellectuals from the two parts of Germany and went so far as to book a place in Switzerland for a residential meeting; but as plans progressed, East German enthusiasm waned. During the Nigeria-Biafra war, the Quaker team made repeated attempts to arrange direct meetings between the two sides at senior or intermediate levels, and Adam Curle explored the use of the Quaker Centre in Geneva as a neutral meeting place; but one side or the other always wanted to impose conditions before talks could begin.[270] The idea of direct talks on Southern Rhodesia (Zimbabwe) was promoted by Friends on more than one occasion in 1979, but the parties were unenthusiastic—though they did eventually come together under official British sponsorship at Lancaster House in London.

After Sadat's visit to Jerusalem in 1977, he and Menachem Begin met a number of times, but these meetings only made the situation worse. After a number of unfortunate direct confrontations at Camp David, President Carter asked the two leaders to negotiate *with him* rather than with each other.[271] It seems to be the case that, if summit meetings are to make progress, they have to be well-prepared, and the timing and setting have to be just right.

The disinterested intermediary may know roughly what issues have to be resolved. What we sometimes fail to understand is that the formulation of the agenda and the order of items may determine the outcome. In 1949, the UN Commission for India and Pakistan proposed that a meeting of the two sides on Kashmir should be held at ministerial level, and a provisional agenda in neutral terms was suggested. Both India and Pakistan agreed to attend the meeting, but both suggested that the agenda be expanded to include items known to be unacceptable to the other side. Neither party would budge, so the idea of a face-to-face meeting had to be abandoned.[272]

The last point I want to deal with in this section is a difficult one.

Roland Warren and Mike Yarrow both stressed the importance of truthfulness in Quaker peace-making: 'nothing can replace a personal quality of transparent honesty.' The London Yearly Meeting *Book of Discipline* states that Friends do not take oaths because to do so sets a double standard of truthfulness, 'whereas sincerity and truth should be practised in all dealings of life.'[273] It is our reputation for truthfulness that undergirds and authenticates the campaign for *Truth and Integrity in Public Affairs*.

There is no prohibition of lying in the Ten Commandments. Indeed, in the Old Testament, deception was sometimes praiseworthy, as when Abraham and Isaac pretended that their wives were their sisters, or when Jacob pretended to be Esau, or when Saul disguised himself when consulting the witch of En-dor. On the other hand, I can think of no case in the New Testament where lying was commended. Indeed, the deception of Ananias and Sapphira led to their deaths.[274]

Are there, then, no circumstances in which we are morally required to deceive? To save someone from slavery, torture, or death? When Levi Coffin and other North American Friends ran the Underground Railroad for fugitive slaves in the middle of the nineteenth century, they often resorted to procrastination, prevarication, and evasion. Fugitive slaves were put in disguised clothes, or questions were answered with other questions. On one occasion, a misleading telegram was sent to a newspaper to put pursuers off the scent. But the Quakers told no deliberate lies.[275]

During the Nazi times, it was sometimes a moral duty to lie. Dietrich Bonhoeffer, the German pacifist who, after much heart-searching, joined the conspiracy to assassinate Hitler, entitled the last and uncompleted chapter of his book on Christian ethics 'What is meant by 'Telling the Truth'?' This was written in 1943 while Bonhoeffer was in the military prison at Tegel. Bonhoeffer maintained that to be truthful is not something that we owe to other human beings but something that we owe to God. Truthfulness 'is not solely a matter of moral character; it is also a matter of correct appreciation of real situations, and of serious reflection upon them.' Eberhard Bethge, Bonhoeffer's friend and biographer, comments enigmatically that the 'confusing content' of this chapter shows us what were the consequences of the anti-Nazi struggle.[276]

Deborah Halfdan-Nielsen, a leading Danish Quaker, was once asked by a policeman during the Nazi occupation if she knew the whereabouts of a Jewish fugitive. She knew very well where this person was hiding, but she answered 'no'. Her daughter, Ellen Friis, writes: 'My mother was a very honest person and had not told a lie easily, but she had not found any other solution at that particular moment.' The finale to the story has a certain poignancy, however, for after the war, the same policeman reproached her for not telling the truth, for he knew that she was a Quaker.[277]

Quaker workers in some situations face painful choices if to tell the truth may expose other people to grave danger. QPS has prepared for Quaker workers a paper of guidance for dealing with these issues. Some Quaker workers consider that our commitment to honesty in word and deed requires us to tell the truth at all times, even if to do so places others at risk: others believe that it is sometimes necessary to deceive in order to protect the fundamental human rights of others. Workers should be warned in advance that such predicaments may arise, and should receive the advice of responsible committees and experienced colleagues.[278]

(iii) The Outcome. The constitution of UNESCO states that wars begin in the human mind (it actually says 'in the minds of men'), so that it is in the human mind that the defences of peace must be constructed. Friends who embark on peace-making do so without outward weapons, but hoping to help the parties to draw on their own inner resources in the search for justice and peace.

Not all Friends have thought this an appropriate Quaker activity, believing that it would be better to concentrate on meeting spiritual needs. This was the view of at least one member of Meeting for Sufferings in 1918 when the unofficial Friends League of Nations Committee wished to approach President Wilson about the proposed international organization to keep the peace. A similar view was expressed by some German Friends during the Nazi times, and some Friends in Southern Rhodesia thought in the 1970s that Friends from abroad should help to deepen the spiritual life of the meetings rather than involve themselves in complex and sensitive political matters. The QPS handbook on mediation notes that work for peace may be difficult in areas where the local Yearly Meeting gives primary attention to evangelism.[279]

Another view is that the traditional and distinctive Quaker role is to relieve human suffering, whether in time of war or in time of peace, and that Friends have no special competence for the complex task of peace-making.

A third view is that Friends should promote peace by lobbying or demonstrating for general goals, but should not concern themselves with detailed technical negotiations between parties in conflict, a process which can easily divert us from our fundamental witness against all outward weapons.

My own view is that if we say 'no' to all war, we have an obligation to do our utmost to prevent it from ever happening. In any case, I cannot be easy with arbitrary divisions among different kinds of Quaker witness. Paul of Tarsus insisted that the completeness of the Christian community requires a diversity of gifts and callings.[280] Every genuine Quaker concern comes from God, and I try not to belittle genuine concerns that differ from my own. Moreover, my review of peace efforts by British Friends over the past two centuries suggests that the strategic aim is to build a world in which outward weapons are not needed to ensure justice, but that tactics must be constantly adapted to meet changing circumstances.

This is not to say that Quaker mediation is easy and without dangers. Friends go into situations of great complexity, situations with a long background of grievance and counter-grievance, and where opinions may be derived from false information or be grotesquely inflated. Both sides would like to have Quaker goodwill and support. We are sometimes given incomplete or even false information in an effort to gain our approval.[281] When we were on a peace mission to the Middle East in 1973, we were told something which we knew wasn't true: were we to remain silent and appear gullible or contradict the official and appear contentious? (We remained silent.) And how are we to respond when one party makes an apparently conciliatory proposal but which we believe is designed, not to serve the cause of peace and justice, but to wrong-foot the other party? This is not unknown in the diplomatic world: the published volumes on US Foreign Relations between 1946 and 1960 give many examples of proposals drafted for the UN Security Council with the deliberate aim of provoking a Soviet veto, and I have been told that there were more than twenty cases between 1960 and 1990 when African states drafted resolutions for the Security Council on Southern Africa with the express intention that one or more of the Western permanent members would veto.

The natural inclination of the Quaker peace-maker is to encourage and strengthen the moderates on each side, the peaceniks. This is a legitimate tactic, but it should not obscure the fact that it is sometimes the more extreme leaders with solid political backing who are able to take risks for peace.[282]

The mediator must try to keep a level head. It is easy to become discouraged when dealing with long-standing and intractable problems, and when the parties fail to see that it is in their long-term interests to make compromises for peace. But an equal danger is to be overly optimistic, to give the parties the impression that the other has made or will make concessions which, on closer examination, turn out to be non-existent. That was a mistake made in May 1983 by the Personal Representative of the UN Secretary-General for Afghanistan (Diego Cordovez), with unfortunate consequences.[283]

Another danger is for the intermediary to manipulate the relations between the parties in the hope of thereby achieving a positive outcome. Henry Kissinger, while engaged in shuttle diplomacy between Israel and the Arab states in May 1974, withheld from Syria some Israeli concessions 'so that he would have something to show on later trips.'[284] This eventually became known in Damascus, thereby reducing Kissinger's usefulness as a mediator.

The origin of each Quaker peace-making exercise is religious concern, what Max Weber would have called an ethic of motive or intention. In reaching a collective decision at the strategic level, we do not have to take account of the likelihood of 'success', for we do not know how to measure 'success' in these matters. Indeed, a crucial advantage for non-official mediators is that they do not need to claim 'success'. Elmore Jackson did not consider that his 1955 mission to the Middle East had achieved 'success'. 'The negotiations had clarified areas of flexibility [and] had developed on both sides a greater understanding of the requirements and possibilities of negotiation.' Yet war followed thirteen months later. The mission which Paul Johnson and I undertook to the Middle East was followed by war seven months later. Mike Yarrow insisted that the Quaker mediator must not only renounce publicity: 'he must also deny himself many elements of ego satisfaction from his efforts.' Adam Curle believes that non-official mediators 'are not going to be able to bring off dramatic coups.' In the complex weave of international affairs, 'there is never *one* person, *one* group, *one* event to which the final result can be attributed.' If the mediator helps the parties to move closer together, it is the parties and not the intermediary who should take the credit.[285]

After all, those in the secular world who try to solve international problems do not chalk up many successes. If one reads the memoirs of Garret FitzGerald (Ireland) or George Ball (USA), of U Thant (Burma and the UN) or Abba Eban (Israel), the impression one receives is of rebuff, frustration, deadlock, setback, and failure, only occasionally of relative triumph or success.

Friends do not engage in peace-making in the expectation of achieving success in outward terms, but out of inner religious concern. Roger Wilson stressed that concern is not simply a matter of 'preferences . . . based on reasoning or inclination.' He defined true concern as 'a gift from God, a leading of his Spirit which may not be denied.'[286]

Mike Yarrow described concern as 'the religiously inspired impulse to put God's love into action in some concrete situation.' The concern of the individual Friend is tested in a group, which (according to Yarrow) has to deal rigorously with such mundane tactical matters as the availability of resources, prior experience in the area, contacts with responsible decision-makers, and knowledge of the main elements in the dispute. 'The Quaker method has the strength of combining the intensity of individual commitment with the tempering of group process. It has the weakness of being cumbersome and uncertain in application.' Indeed, 'a concern ignored by one Quaker body may bring inspired support from another.'[287]

There is a passage in the book of Isaiah that reads:

Also I heard the voice of the Lord, saying,
Whom shall I send, and who will go for us?
Then said I, Here am I; send me.[288]

We have had a joke in our family that it is *not* a true concern if one says, 'Here am I; send Duncan Wood.'* Ted Milligan has stressed that it is alien to the Quaker and Christian tradition to have 'concerns' that *other* people should do certain work.[289]

The Society of Friends disposes of limited resources of personnel and money. Even to decide to reject a proposal for new work takes the time of staff and committees. There are many needed things that Quakers cannot do, and it is a sign of maturity to be able to say 'no' graciously.

*Duncan Wood was one of my colleagues in the FAU in China. He and his wife Katharine represented the Quaker service agencies at the UN in Geneva for many years.

Quaker Peace and Service has established guidelines for assessing proposals for new work. Some of these I have already referred to (authentic concern, previous humanitarian service in the area, the agreement or involvement of local Friends, the availability of qualified personnel able to undertake open-ended assignments, whether there are other official or non-governmental agencies as well or better qualified to undertake the task). Other guidelines apply more to humanitarian service than to peace-making.

There are, however, two guidelines which might be relevant to Quaker mediation and reconciliation but which we have not yet discovered how to apply in a consistent way: a feasible procedure for evaluation, and the possibility that eventually the work should be handed over to local auspices. Maybe we have been negligent in not taking these two guidelines more seriously, but my own belief is that we need more written case-studies of Quaker peace-making before we can refine and apply these two criteria. I hope I have learned from my own mistakes: what I have hardly begun to do is to learn from the mistakes of my Quaker colleagues.

When a Friend is asked to help resolve a conflict, he or she is likely to feel pleased, even flattered, but this is not the same as religious concern. It is here that the role of colleagues becomes crucial, for it is their task to ask penetrating questions, to relate this opportunity to other demands on Quaker resources, to decide when to pursue an objective in spite of setbacks and when to pause for a while so that the parties may re-assess their objectives or other agencies may try their hand. It is essential to clarify aims at the beginning of each operation, but the situation is moving all the time, and aims may have to be modified in the light of changing circumstances.

Friends have always been active in the peace research movement. The pioneer was Lewis Richardson (1881–1953); and, in our own day, Kenneth Boulding in the United States and Adam Curle in Britain have kept the subject alive. It is not to belittle the work that has been done so far to assert that we still do not know much about how to build a peaceful and just world, though Friends are convinced that the use of outward weapons cannot be the best way. Quaker peace-making is based on religious concern rather than scientific laws and principles.

Some Quaker aims have been successfully achieved in times past, like the abolition of the slave trade in the British Empire. World peace is not like that. In the foreseeable future, we shall not reach that goal.

Work for peace, as Horace Alexander stressed, is a lifetime occupation. We have still much to learn and much to do.[290]

PEACE IS A PROCESS TO ENGAGE IN, NOT A GOAL TO BE REACHED

Friends take seriously some of the hard sayings of Jesus, but not all of them. Few of us refrain from taking thought for the morrow; most of us have, in a modest way, laid up treasure on earth. I know of no Friends who have sold *all* that they have and given the proceeds to the poor.[291]

Much that Jesus told his followers can be found in the moral teaching of his contemporaries; in the main Jewish sects (Pharisees, Sadducees, Essenes), in the Qumran community, in Greek philosophy, in Roman law. But it seems to me that in two respects the teaching of Jesus was unique. First, his stress on the primacy of unconditional love: love of God, love of neighbour, love for tax collectors and prostitutes, even love of enemy. Second, his insistence that all human beings are of equal worth, so that there are to be no barriers derived from gender, national origin, skin colour, social status, political allegiance, sexual orientation, or other arbitrary distinction.

The follower of Jesus is to discover and then promote the Kingdom of God. That Kingdom has two tenses: it is already here, in each one of us; and it is still to come, when God's goodness becomes a universal norm. We are to live now 'as if' the Kingdom of God were already fulfilled.[292]

Peace begins within ourselves. It is to be implemented within the family, in our Meetings, in our work and leisure, in our own localities, and internationally. The task will never be done. Peace is a process to engage in, not a goal to be reached.

REFERENCES

1 For a full exposition of King-Hall's views, see *Defence in the Nuclear Age*, London, Gollancz, 1958, esp. pp.10, 13–4, 23, 38, 145, 190, 196, 223

2 *Summa Theologica*, 11/11, question 40, art.1

3 *Church Government*, LYM, 1968, §834

4 George Fox, *Journal*, ed. by John L. Nickalls, Cambridge University Press, 1952, p.65

5 *The Friend*, 2nd month 1846, pp.24–5

6 Fox (see note 4), pp.398–404

7 James 4: 1–2

8 Robert Barclay, *Apology for the True Christian Divinity*, Proposition XV, sections XIII–XV

9 Edward Burrough, *The Memorable Works . . .*, 1672, pp.537–40

10 Isaac Penington, *Somewhat spoken to a Weighty Question . . .* , 1661, p.8

11 Robert Barclay, *Apology*, Proposition XV, section XV

12 *Minutes of the Provincial Council of Pennsylvania*, 1851–2, vol. IV, p.366; *Pennsylvania Archives*, 1st series, vol. II, p.516

13 Robert Barclay, *Apology*, Proposition XV, section XV; Jonathan Dymond, *Essays on the Principles of Morality*, 1829, vol. I, pp.464–6; E. St. John Catchpool, *Candles in the Darkness*, London, Bannisdale Press, 1966, p.61

14 Joshua 6: 1–20

15 William Penn, *A Brief Account of the Rise and Progress of the People called Quakers*, 1694, p.40

16 William C. Braithwaite, *The Second Period of Quakerism*, Cambridge University Press, revised ed., 1961, p.601; London Yearly Meeting, *Epistle*, 1693; *A Journal of the Life of Thomas Story*, Newcastle-upon-Tyne, 1747, p.125

17 William Penn, *No Cross, No Crown*, 1682, p.57

18 Penn, in a letter to James Harrison, 25 August 1681; see Edwin B. Bronner, *William Penn's 'Holy Experiment'*, New York and London, Temple University Publications, 1962, pp.6, 269–70

19 *Minutes of the Provincial Council of Pennsylvania*, vol. I, pp.299, 300, 306, 309

20 *Ibid.*, pp.399–400, 415, 426–8, 431–3; Bronner (see note 18), pp.160–2

21 *Minutes of the Provincial Council of Pennsylvania*, Vol. II, pp.449, 452, 459, 460, 463, 466–7; *Pennsylvania Archives*, vol. II, pp.857–81; *Correspondence between William Penn and James Logan . . .* , ed. by Edward Armstrong, Philadelphia, 1870, pp.346–7, 350; Isaac Sharpless, *A Quaker Experiment in Government*, Philadelphia, 1898, pp.198–202

22 *Minutes of the Provincial Council of Pennsylvania*, vol. I, pp.493–5; vol. II, pp.24, 30–1, 35, 40–1; *Pennsylvania Archives*, 1st series, vol. I, p.192; Sharpless (see note 21), pp.196–7

23 Public Record Office, files CO5/1233/182041, 12 July 1694, and CO5/1114/182041, 21 August 1694; Sharpless (see note 21), pp.193–4

24 *Ibid.*, pp.206–11

25 *Minutes of the Provincial Council of Pennsylvania*, vol. VI, pp.1–3, 49; *Pennsylvania Archives*, vol. II, pp.189, 516–9

26 *The Journal and Major Essays of John Woolman*, ed. by Phillips P. Moulton, New York, Oxford University Press, 1971, pp.50, 82–87

27 *Chain of Friendship: Selected Letters of Dr John Fothergill of London, 1735–1780*, ed. by

Betsy C. Corner and Christopher C. Booth, Cambridge, Mass., Harvard University Press, 1971, pp.70–1, 165–6, 169

28 George Crosfield, *Memoirs of the Life and Gospel Labours of Samuel Fothergill*, 1843, pp.241–2, 247, 255

29 Corner and Booth (see note 27), pp.174–5

30 London Yearly Meeting Minutes, 1756, vol. II, pp.112–3; Meeting for Sufferings Minutes, vol 30, p.1; Meeting for Sufferings Papers, 1755–57; Corner and Booth (see note 27), p.179

31 Sharpless (see note 21), pp.252–9, 264

32 Carl Heath, *Religion and Public Life* (Swarthmore Lecture 1922), Birmingham, Woodbrooke Extension Committee, 1922, pp.53, 54, 64

33 Konrad Braun, *Justice and the law of Love* (Swarthmore Lecture 1950), London, Allen and Unwin, 1950, p.59

34 Job Scott, *Journal of the Life, Travels and Gospel Labours*, London, 1843, p.66

35 Joshua Maule, *Transactions and Changes in the Society of Friends . . .* , Philadelphia, 1886, pp.219, 317

36 *Ibid.*, pp.220–4, 226, 233–51, 261–7, 271, 284–5

37 For a fair-minded account of Friends' efforts from a legal point of view, see Nicholas Grief, 'British Quakers, the Peace Tax and International Law', in *The Influence of Religion on the Development of International Law*, ed. by Mark W. Janis, Dordrecht (Netherlands), Nijhoff, 1991, pp.243–60

38 Willis H. Hall, *Quaker International Work in Europe since 1914*, Chambery, Imprimeries Réunies, 1938, pp.70–1

39 John W. Graham, *Conscription and Conscience*, London, Allen and Unwin, 1922, pp.349, 352; Margaret E. Hirst, *The Quakers in Peace and War*, London, Swarthmore Press: New York, Doran, 1923, p.538

40 Roger C. Wilson, *Authority, Leadership and Concern* (Swarthmore Lecture 1949), London, Allen and Unwin, 1949, p.6

41 D. Owen Stephens, *With the Quakers in France*, London, Daniel, 1921, p.232

42 Wilson (see note 40), p.9

43 Denis Hayes, *Challenge of Conscience*, London, Allen and Unwin, 1949, pp.382–3

44 *The Friend*, 29 January 1943, p.76; 19 March 1943, pp.201–3; and 26 March 1943, p.220

45 Rufus M. Jones, *The Quakers in the American Colonies*, London, Macmillan, 1911, pp.392–3

46 Hirst (see note 39), pp.226–32; Peter Brock, *The Quaker Peace Testimony, 1660–1914*, York, Sessions Book Trust, 1990, pp.41–2

47 Hirst (see note 39), pp.233–40; London Yearly Meeting *Proceedings*, 1858, p.103

48 Hirst (see note 39), pp.189, 259; Brock (see note 46), pp.35, 270–1; Michael McGarvie, *The Book of Street*, Buckingham, Barracuda Books in association with C. and J. Clark Ltd., 1987, p.128

49 *Apology*, Proposition XV, section XIII.

50 [William Rathbone], *A Narrative of Events that have lately taken place in Ireland . . .* , London, 1804, pp.50–1 and Appendix II, pp.16–27

51 Thomas Foster, *A Narrative of the Proceedings . . . in the case of Hannah Barnard*, London, 1804, pp.XIII, 5, 9–10; see also Rufus Jones, *The Later Periods of Quakerism*, Macmillan, 1921, vol. I, pp.299–305

52 LYM, *Christian Faith and Practice* . . . , 1960, §s199, 200, 203 and 204
53 *From Max Weber: Essays in Sociology*, ed. by H. H. Gerth and C. Wright Mills, London, Routledge, 1948, pp.120–6; Romans 3: 8
54 C. H. 'Mike' Yarrow, *Quaker Experiences in International Conciliation*, New Haven, Yale University Press, 1978, p.298
55 Roger C. Wilson, *Relief and Reconstruction*, Pendle Hill Pamphlet, no.22, Wallingford , Pa., 1943, pp.13–4
56 *Four Quartets*, 'Burnt Norton', pt.1
57 George S. Brookes, *Friend Anthony Benezet*, Philadelphia, University of Pennsylvania Press, 1937, pp.60–75
58 John Ormerod Greenwood, *Quaker Encounters*, York, Sessions, 1975, vol. I, p.4; Hirst (see note 39), pp.392–3
59 Greenwood (see note 58), vol. I, pp.12–7; vol. II, pp.86–7; Hirst (see note 39), pp.475–7; Brock (see note 46), pp.236–7
60 William Allen, *Life* . . . , 1846/9, vol. II, pp.60–3, 103–4, 107, 131 of the London ed. (pp.266–70, 323–5, 328, 360 of the Philadelphia ed.); *First Report of a Committee . . . for the Relief of Distressed Greeks*, 1824; Greenwood (see note 58), vol. I, pp.19–21
61 *Report of the Committee for the Relief of Famine in Finland*, 1858; Henry Richard, *Memoirs of Joseph Sturge*, 1864; pp.506–16; Alexandrina Peckover, *Life of Joseph Sturge*, London, Swan Sonnenschein, 1890, pp.126–131; Stephen Hobhouse, *Joseph Sturge*, London, Dent, 1919, pp.158–61; Sarah G. Harvey, *Memorials of Thomas Harvey*, printed for private circulation, 1886, pp.21–4; Richenda C. Scott, *Quakers in Russia*, London, Michael Joseph, 1964, pp.127–30
62 For this and subsequent paragraphs on the Friends War Victims Relief Fund in the Franco-Prussian War, see John Bellows, *The Track of War Around Metz*, London, 1870; Robert Spence Watson, *Villages Around Metz*, Newcastle upon Tyne, 1870; James Hack Tuke, *A Visit to Paris in the Spring of 1871* . . . , London, 1871; Samuel James Capper, *Wanderings in war time*, London 1871, pp.93–255, 283–98, 321–34; James Long, *Rapport de la Répartition des Secours faite par la Société des Amis (Quakers) aux Innocentes Victimes de la Guerre en France* (1870–1871), Paris, 1872; William Jones, *Quaker Campaigns in Peace and War*, London, 1899, pp.75–192; (This book was re-published as *Reminiscences of the Franco-German War of 1870* by the Peace Society, London, in 1914); Elizabeth Bellows, *John Bellows: Letters and Memoir*, London, Kegan Paul, 1904, pp.14–22; William K Sessions, *They Chose the Star*, York, Sessions Book Trust, 2nd ed., 1991; Greenwood (see note 58), vol. I, p.49. Thirteen reports of the Committee covering the period 2 November 1870–19 August 1871 are in the Library at Friends House
63 For this and subsequent paragraphs about relief during the Anglo-Boer war, see S. E. Robson, *Joshua Rowntree*, London, Allen and Unwin, 1916, pp.110–23; Hope Hay Hewison, *Hedge of Wild Almonds*, London, Currey, 1989, pp.98, 163–5, 190–1, 205–24, 242–61, 273–4, 313–4; Phone conversations with Hope Hay Hewison, 16 July and 9 August and letter of 4 September 1991; Howard Evans, *Sir Randal Cremer*, London, Fisher Unwin, 1909, pp.208–23
64 Tuke (see note 62), p.15
65 Meeting for Sufferings, Minutes, vol. 56 (1912–1916), 4 September 1914, Minute 3
66 For this and subsequent paragraphs about the Friends War Victims Relief Committee in the first world war, see A. Ruth Fry, *A Quaker Adventure*, London, Nisbet,

1926; Stephens (see note 41); Francesca M. Wilson, *In the Margins of Chaos*, London, Murray, 1924, pp.3, 9–14; Catchpool (see note 13), pp.19–72, Alex Bryan, 'A Friends Relief Service worker looks back', *Friends Quarterly*, vol. 20, no.4 (October 1977), pp.159–64; Rufus Jones, *A Service of Love in War-time*, New York, Macmillan, 1920; Lester M. Jones, *Quakers in Action*, New York, Macmillan, 1929, pp.18–36, 121–8; Mary Hoxie Jones, *Swords into Ploughshares*, New York, Macmillan, 1937, pp.12–74; Greenwood (see note 58), vol. I, pp.179 n.1, 181, 194–214; Graham (see note 39), p.349, Scott (see note 61), pp.148–225

67 Anna Braithwaite Thomas, *St. Stephens House*, London, Friends Emergency Committee, 1921; Hirst (see note 39), pp.494–7; Greenwood (see note 58), vol. I, pp.180, 214–8; Vol. III, p.189

68 London Yearly Meeting *Proceedings*, 1916, pp.145–6

69 Meaburn Tatham and James E. Miles (eds.), *The Friends Ambulance Unit, 1914–1919*, London, Swarthmore Press, 1920; H. Lidbetter and N. Monk-Jones, *SSA. 14*, printed for private circulation by J. Ellis Benson, 1919; Corder Catchpool, *On two fronts*, London , Allen and Unwin, 3rd ed., 1940, pp.20–83, 88–96, 131–3, 145, 155; E. St John Catchpool (see note 13), pp.19–23; Hirst (see note 39), pp.501–3, 510–1; Graham (see note 39), pp.97, 157–9, 346–7; Greenwood (see note 58), 179–93

70 Roger C. Wilson, *Quaker Relief*, London, Allen and Unwin, 1953, pp.127–8, 168–72; Wilson (see note 66), pp.236–67; Greenwood (see note 58), pp.313–5

71 Lawrence Darton, *An Account of the Work of the Friends Committee for Refugees and Aliens, first known as the German Emergency Committee of the Society of Friends, 1933–1950*, 1954 (mimeo.); Elsie F. Howard, *Across Barriers*, Buckhurst Hill (Essex), Chigwell Press, 1941, pp.33–127; Elsie F. Howard, *Midstream*, London, Friends Book Centre, 1945, pp.109–30; Elsie F. Howard, *Barriers Down*, London, Home Service Committee, 1950, p.16; William R. Hughes, *Indomitable Friend*, London, Housmans, 1964, pp.103–4; letter from Anna Sabine Halle, 7 December 1991; Hall (see note 38), pp.160–7

72 The text of the letter is in Darton (see note 71), pp.155–7

73 Meeting for Sufferings, Minutes Vol. 62, 5 July 1935, Minute 3; *The Friend*, 12 July 1935, p.639

74 For this and subsequent paragraphs on the FAU, see A. Tegla Davies, *Friends Ambulance Unit*, London, Allen and Unwin, 1947; Wilson (see note 70), pp.5, 329–34; Clarence E. Pickett, *For more than bread*, Boston, Mass., Little, Brown, 1953, pp.211–23, 246–52; Greenwood (see note 58), pp.277–308

75 Phone conversation with Bob McClure, 9 August 1991

76 Letter from Duncan Wood, 22 August 1991

77 Meeting for Sufferings, Minutes, Vol. 63, (1938–1941), 1 November 1940, Minute 4

78 For this and subsequent paragraphs on FRS, see Wilson (see note 70), esp. pp.23–33; Wilson (see note 40), esp. pp.32–72; Darton (see note 71), pp.114–8; Greenwood (see note 58), vol. III, pp.309–26

79 London Yearly Meeting *Proceedings*, 1944, Minute 3

80 Letter from John Saunders, 3 August 1991

81 Wilson (see note 40), p.13

82 Pickett (see note 74), p.95; Duncan Wood, 'A History of Quaker International Peacemaking Efforts', in *New Call to Peacemaking*, ed. by Norval Hadley, Philadelphia, Friends World Committee for Consultation, 1976, p.63

83 Catchpool (see note 13), p.48
84 'Workers with God', *Friends Quarterly Examiner*, vol. 80, no.318 (April 1946), p.116
85 Pickett (see note 74), p.292
86 *Ibid.*, pp.134–5, 285
87 Wilson (see note 66), p.270
88 UN General Assembly resolution 187 (S-2), 6 May 1948; Pablo de Azcárate, *Mission in Palestine, 1948–1952*, Washington D. C., Middle East Institute, 1966, p.50
89 Ramses Nassif, *U Thant in New York, 1961–1971*, London, Hurst, 1988, pp.3–4
90 London Yearly Meeting, *Epistle*, 1847, p.3
91 Henry van Etten (see note 84), p.116
92 Meeting for Sufferings, Minutes, Vol. 28, pp.342, 350, 372–3, 378–80 (15 May, 12 June, 4 and 25 September and 2 October 1748)
93 *Ibid.*, vol. 46, pp.376, 380–5, 391–2 (6, 11 and 17 January and 25 February 1854); Richard (see note 61), pp.463–72, 605–6; Peckover (see note 61), pp.110–21; Hobhouse (see note 61), pp.141–9; Anna F. Fox, *Memoir of Robert Charleton*, 2nd ed., London, 1976, pp.61–78; Mary H. Pease, *Henry Pease, A short story of his life*, London, 1897, pp.48–56; Stephen Frick, 'The Quaker Deputation to Russia: January-February 1854', *Journal of the Friends Historical Society*, vol. 52, no.2 (1969), pp.78–96
94 Richard (see note 61), pp.474–8; Frick (see note 93), pp.79–88; Pease (see note 93), pp.56–65
95 Frick (see note 93), pp.79–80
96 The Minutes of the Friends League of Nations Committee are deposited in the Library at Friends House, London
97 *The Friend*, 10 January 1919, pp.15–6
98 The text is printed in *The Friend*, 24 January 1919
99 I have used the facsimile of the original edition published by Olms-Weidmann in 1983: references to the Everyman edition are in parenthesis.
100 *Ibid.*, pp.43–61 (pp.15–20)
101 *Ibid.*, pp.11–5 (pp.6–7)
102 *Ibid.*, pp.16–9, 26–30 (pp.7–8, 10–1)
103 *Ibid.*, pp.30–5 (pp.11–12)
104 *Ibid.*, pp.35–43 (pp.13–5)
105 *Ibid.*, pp.62–7 (pp.20–2)
106 The full text of the plan is in *John Bellers: his life, times and writings*, ed. by George Clark, London, Routledge, 1987: extracts are in *John Bellers, 1654–1725*, ed. by A. Ruth Fry, London, Cassell, 1935. In the following notes, I refer to the page numbers of the Clarke edition, with the Fry page numbers in parenthesis.
107 *Ibid.*, pp.141–2 (pp.94–5)
108 *Ibid.*, pp.137, 140 (pp.92–3)
109 *Ibid.*, pp.137, 140–1, 150, 152–3 (pp.91–4, 99, 103)
110 *Ibid.*, pp.134, 145, 148, 151 (pp.89, 98–9, 101)
111 Titus 2: 1–14; Colossians 3: 18–22; James 1: 27
112 London Yearly Meeting Minutes, vol. XX, 1783, pp.299–300; Meeting for Sufferings Minutes, vol. 37, 11 June 1784, p.62; London Yearly Meeting Minutes, 1784, pp.446–7
113 Allen (see note 60), Vol. I, pp.191, 224, 297, 302, 330, 353 (143, 167, 222, 225, 247,

264); George Eaton, *Joseph Tregelles Price . . .* , Neath, Glamorgan Press, 1987, pp.23–4; Richard (see note 61), pp.415, 428, 565, 568; Hirst (see note 39), pp.243–4

114 Evans (see note 63), pp.59–63

115 *The Letters of Queen Victoria*, ed. by A. C. Benson and Viscount Esher, London, Murray, 1907, vol. III, p.446

116 H. J. Leech (ed.), *The Public Letters of the Rt. Hon. John Bright*, 2nd ed. 1895, 'I would advise you not to trouble yourself with the abstract question. The practical question is the one that presses', *Ibid.*, p.25

117 [Sir George Newman], 'Recollections of Lord Gainford', *Friends Quarterly Examiner*, vol. 77, no.306, 1943, pp.115–6

118 William I. Hull, *The Two Hague Conferences*, Boston, Ginn, 1908 (for the International School of Peace), p.471; Elizabeth Balmer Baker and P. J. Noel-Baker, *J. Allen Baker*, London, Swarthmore Press, 1927, pp.123–4, 141–205, 227–31, 241–2

119 A. C. F. Beales, *The History of Peace*, London, Bell, 1931, p.159; Warren F. Kuehl, *Seeking world order*, Nashville, Vanderbilt University Press, 1969, pp.38, 163

120 For this and the following paragraph, see J. E. G. de Montmorency, *Francis William Fox*, Oxford University Press, 1923, pp.19–20, 95, 130–3; *The Annual Monitor for 1919–20*, pp.114–25; Evans (see note 63); *Memoirs of Bertha von Suttner*, Boston, Ginn, 1910 (for the International School of Peace), vol. I, p.301; vol. II, pp.58–9. 373, 375, 413–4; William Jones (see note 62), pp.260–5, 268–9, 280, 404; Beales (see note 119), pp.189–90

121 Larry E. Burgess, *Mohonk: Its People and Spirit*, New Paltz, NY, Smiley Bros. Inc., 1980, pp.46–9; Kuehl (see note 119), pp.40–1, 66, 71, 78–80, 93, 110–1, 115, 117, 124, 144, 190–1, 244; Beales (see note 119), p.245

122 For an extract from the deed establishing the Endowment for International Peace, in Carnegie's inimitable spelling, see my *War and Conscience in the Nuclear Age*, London, Macmillan, 1987, p.119; also Evans (see note 63), p.124

123 Suttner (see note 120), vol. II, pp.249, 278, 286

124 Frederick W. Holls, *The Peace Conference [of 1899] at The Hague*, London, Macmillan, 1900, pp.66–92; Hull (see note 118), pp.52–75, 449–50, 456–7; James Scott Brown, *The Hague Peace Conferences of 1899 and 1907*, Baltimore, Johns Hopkins Press, 1909, vol. I, pp.54–7, 654–72; vol. II, pp.77, 289; Joseph H. Choate, *The Two Hague Conferences*, Princeton University Press: London, Oxford University Press, 1913, pp.8–12; Agnes Fry, *Memoir of the Right Honourable Sir Edward Fry*, Oxford University Press, 1921, pp.203–6; Suttner (see note 120), vol. II, pp.267–8, 284– 5, 291–3, 304–13, 324–6

125 Holls (see note 124), pp.164–305; Hull (see note 118), pp.267–448, 454–6, 461–3, 470–6, 490–6; Brown (see note 124), vol. I, pp.66–82, 254–312, 319–85, 423–60; vol. II, pp.81–109, 287–355; Choate (see note 124), pp19–24, 27–8, 30–8, 77–82; Fry (see note 124), p.194

126 Letters from Stephen Cary, 20 November and 5 December 1991; Barry Hollister, 22 November 1991; Keith Smiley, 25 November 1991

127 Hull (see note 124), p.17; Suttner (see note 120) vol. II, p.327; Fry (see note 124), pp.202, 213

128 For this and the next paragraph, see Baker (see note 118), pp.206–226; Nils Karlström, 'Movements for International Friendship, Life and Work 1910–1925' in *A History of the Ecumenical Movement, 1517–1948*, ed. by Ruth Rouse and Stephen Charles Neill,London, SPCK, 1954, pp.511–518, 530– 1, 560–8

129 *The Friend*, 20 April 1917, p.298

130 2nd ed., Carl Heath, Oxted, Surrey, [1917]; see also Carl Heath, *The Quaker Centre*, London, Friends Service Council, 1939

131 London Yearly Meeting *Proceedings*, 1918, minute 17

132 London Yearly Meeting *Proceedings*, 1919, minute 44

133 London Yearly Meeting *Proceedings*, 1924, p.24

134 London Yearly Meeting *Proceedings*, 1935, pp.65–6; Horace G. Alexander, 'The Position in the Saar', *The Friend*, 15 February 1935, p.141

135 *Friends in Europe*, ed. by Christina Yates, London, FWCC, 1946, pp.13, 36, 101; Darton (see note 71), pp.58, 114 n.1; Greenwood (see note 58), vol. 3, pp.155–6, 280, 294

136 On this particular aspect, see Hall (see note 38), pp.105–8; Bertram Pickard, *Pacifist Diplomacy in Conflict Situations*, Philadelphia, Pacifist Research Bureau, 1943, p.29

137 Howard, *Across Barriers*, (see note 71), pp.12–32; Howard, *Midstream*, (see note 71) pp.84–98; Joan Mary Fry, *In Downcast Germany*, London, 1944; Hughes (see note 71), pp. 68–162; Leonard S. Kenworthy, *An American Quaker inside Nazi Germany*, Kennett Square (Pa.), Quaker Publications, 1982; Darton (see note 71), pp.12–5, 56–7, 66; Hall (see note 38), pp.145–56. 194–5; *Friends in Europe* (see note 135), p.47; Greenwood (see note 58), vol. 3, pp.305–12

138 Hall (see note 38), pp.127, 193–4; Darton (see note 71), pp.21, 56

139 There is a typed report on the Vienna Centre, 1922–37, by Headley Horsnail, in the Library at Friends House; see esp. pp.14–6, 42, 45–82. See also Helen Fox, 'Friends' International Service: the Vienna Centre', *The Friend*, 28 October 1921, pp.717–8

140 *Friends in Europe* (see note 135), pp.4, 34, 64; Kenworthy (see note 137), pp.35–7; Hughes (see note 71), pp.148–9; Hall (see note 38), pp.162, 185, 195; Darton (see note 71), pp.45–8, 50–2, 66; Greenwood (see note 58), vol. 3, pp.249–54

141 Scott (see note 61), pp.263–72; Hall (see note 38) , pp.189, 191–3

142 Hall (see note 38), pp.145–7, 156, 181, 188; *Friends in Europe* (see note 135), p.51

143 Ethel Jones, 'Friends' International Service: the Geneva Centre', *The Friend*, 1 July 1921, pp.424–5; Hall (see note 38), pp.100, 104, 179, 182–4, 195–6; *Friends in Europe* (see note 135), pp.60–1; Greenwood (see note 58), vol. 3, pp.275, 316–9

144 *Ibid.*, p.239

145 Hughes (see note 71), p147

146 Wilson (see note 70), pp12–3; Wilson (see note 40), pp.9–10

147 Friends Peace Committee, 29 June/1 July 1946, minute 7; see also Geoffrey M. Wilson, 'Friction and Fact', *The Friend*, 25 October 1946, pp.857–8

148 Meeting for Sufferings, 31 March 1950, minutes 1 and 8; 5 May 1950, minute 1; *The Friend*, 7 April 1950, pp.252–3

149 Peter Calvocoressi and Sheila Harden (eds.), *Survey of International Affairs, 1949–50*, Oxford University Press, 1953, pp.57–61; Peter Calvocoressi and Konstanze Isepp (eds.), *Survey of International Affairs, 1951*, Oxford University Press, 1954, pp.159–62

150 East West Relations Group, 8 May 1951, minute 158; Kathleen Lonsdale (ed.), *Quakers Visit Russia*, London, Friends Peace Committee, no date but 1951 or 1952, pp.12–3

151 *Ibid.*, esp. pp.2–3, 5–6, 36, 52, 108–13

152 *Ibid.*, pp.118–9

153 *Ibid.*, pp.119–26

154 *Manchester Guardian*, 23 June 1952, p.6

155 Irene Harrison, *Agatha Harrison*, London, Allen and Unwin, 1956, pp.152–5

156 For this and subsequent paragraphs, see *Quakers Visit China*, London, East West Relations and Peace Committees, no date but probably 1956; see also Grigor McClelland, *Quaker Mission to China* (privately printed)

157 For this and subsequent paragraphs, see the articles in *The Friend*, 20 September 1957, pp.845–6, and 11 October 1957, pp.904–7

158 John Miller, *No Cloak, No Dagger*, London, East-West Relations Committee, 1965, esp.pp.1–20, 56

159 'Quakers visit Tito's land', *American Friend*, 18 January 1951, p.20; *Meeting the Russians*, Philadelphia, American Friends Service Council (AFSC), 1956; *Journey through a wall*, Philadelphia, AFSC, [1964]; *Cuba ten years after*, Philadelphia, AFSC, 1970; *Experiment without precedent*, AFSC, 1972 (mimeo.). For a perceptive account of the visit to the two German states, see Yarrow (see note 54), pp.70–90

160 Richard K. Ullmann, 'A Christian Peace Conference', *The Friend*, 15 May 1959, pp.627–8; Ullmann, *The Dilemmas of a Reconciler*, Wallingford, Pa., Pendle Hill pamphlet No.131, 1963; Miller (see note 118), pp.44–7

161 The British Council of Churches published the report of a working party on Eastern Europe, *Discretion and Valour*, by Trevor Beeson, London, Collins, 1974

162 Meeting for Sufferings, Minutes, Vol. 65, 2 March 1945, minute 7

163 Meeting for Sufferings, Minutes, Vol. 56, 10 October 1920, minute 7; *The Friend*, 14 January 1921, p.21

164 General Assembly resolution 362(IV), 22 October 1949. It is now rule 62; Pickett (see note 74), p.410

165 *Ibid.*, pp.405–6, 415; Yarrow (see note 54), pp.43–6

166 Quaker UN Program Committee, 20 January 1958, minute BQH 5(b)

167 UN General Assembly resolution 1155(XII), 26 November 1957

168 Quaker UN Program Committee, 19 November 1956, minute BQH 54; 17 December 1956, minute BQH 95; 21 January 1957, minute BQH 8; 18 February 1957, minute BQH 16

169 Elmore Jackson, *Meeting of Minds*, New York, McGraw-Hill, 1952

170 AFSC, *Future Development . . .* , 1955

171 Pickett (see note 74), pp.407–18; Harrison (see note 155), pp.138–51; Yarrow (see note 54), p.45

172 Quaker UN Program Committee, 16 April 1956, minutes

173 Pickard (see note 136), p.27

174 *Yugoslavia and Peace*, London, National Peace Council, [1950]; 'Inside Yugoslavia Today', *The Friend* 27 October 1950, pp.785–7

175 Tony Benn, *Office without power*, London, Hutchinson, 1988, p.388; *Against the tide*, London, Hutchinson, 1989, pp.310, 691–2; *Conflict of interests*, London, Hutchinson, 1990, pp.267, 569; letter from Sir John Lawrence, 20 November 1991

176 UN docs. E/CN.4/NGO/1/Add.1, 21 March 1950; E/CN.4/NGO.11, 17 April 1950; E/CN.4/SR.161, 19 April 1950

177 UN doc. E/CN.4/Sub.2/200/Rev.1, 1960, pp.43–4

178 UN Commission of Human Rights, 43rd session, resolution 46, 10 March 1987

179 Quaker UN Program Committee, 20 January 1958, minute BQH 6

180 *Chinese Representation in the Security Council and the General Assembly of the United Nations*, Brighton, Institute for the Study of International Organization, 1970

181 UN General Assembly resolution 2758(XXVI), 25 October 1971

182 Gideon Rafael, *Destination Peace*, London, Weidenfeld and Nicolson, 1981, p.38; 'The Orbach File', *New Outlook*, October 1974, pp.6–23, and November–December 1974, pp.8–21

183 Quaker House Committee, 27 January 1955, minute BQH 1(6), and 28 February 1955, minute BQH 13(c)

184 Yarrow (see note 54), pp.118–122

185 Letter from Sylvain Minault, 15 November 1991

186 Letters from Stephen Cary, 20 November 1991, and Larry Ingle, 27 September 1988

187 I have published a full account of this episode in the *Journal of the Friends' Historical Society*, vol. 56, no.2 (1991), pp.148–61, based on the rather scanty records in the archives of the Library at Friends House (and my own recollections) plus the full archives of the Foreign Office in the Public Record Office at Kew

188 The letter can be found in file F0371 99589/FK1071/626 at the Public Record Office

189 First ed., published by the AFSC in Philadelphia and by the two London Committees in April 1970; revised ed. by Fawcett World Library, New York, November 1970; also published in Hebrew, Arabic, and French editions. See also Maureen E. Berman and Joseph E. Johnson (eds.), *Unofficial Diplomats*, New York, Columbia University Press, 1977, pp.81–3; John W. McDonald, Jr. and Diane B. Bendahmane, (eds.), *Conflict Resolution: Track Two Diplomacy*, Washington, D.C., Foreign Service Institute, 1987, pp.58–9

190 Yarrow, (see note 54), pp.227–30, 275–6; Walter Martin, ' "Quaker Diplomacy" as Peace Witness', *The Friend*, 3 August 1984, p.975

191 Ullmann, *Dilemmas of a Reconciler* (see note 160), p.3

192 For this and subsequent paragraphs on the India Reconciliation Group, see Hugh Tinker, 'The India Conciliation Group, 1931–1950: dilemmas of the mediator', *Journal of Commonwealth and Comparative Politics*, vol. XIV, no.3 (1976), pp.224–41; Yarrow (see note 54), pp.145–51; Harrison (see note 155), pp.76–130; Horace Alexander, *The Growth of the peace testimony of the Society of Friends*, London, Quaker Peace and Service, 1982 ed., p.22; Pickard (see note 136), pp.28–9

193 *Foreign Relations of the United States*, 1952–4, vol. XI, p.1645

194 Lonsdale (see note 150), pp.17, 24–8

195 Letter from Herman Backman, 9 October 1991

196 *The Friend*, 14 August 1953, p.760; *The Wayfarer*, November 1953, pp.172–4

197 *A Visit to Moscow*, London, Christian Action, 1955 (mimeo.).

198 'Pray for the Peace of Jerusalem', *World Issues*, no.24 (1972), pp.4–5

199 UN General Assembly Official Records, 46th session, Supplement no.33 (A/46/33), pp.60–72

200 Catchpool (see note 69), pp.55–72

201 For reports of UN observers, see UN Security Council Official Records, 10th year, Supplement for January to March 1955, pp.35–61; E. L. M. Burns, *Between Arab and Israeli*, London, Harrap, 1962, pp.17–21; E. H. Hutchinson, *Violent Truce*, New York, Devin-Adair, 1956, pp.115–20

202 Elmore Jackson, *Middle East Mission*, New York and London, Norton, 1983, pp.26–34; Quaker House Committee, 28 March 1955, minute BQH 26; 25 April 1955, minute BQH 30; 23 May 1955, minute BQH 37(c)

203 Jackson (see note 202), p.78

204 *Ibid.*, pp.35–9, 78, 81, 83–5; see also Rafael (see note 182), p.42

205 Burns (see note 201), pp.76–8

206 *Foreign Relations of the United States*, 1955–57, vol. XIV, p.402; Jackson (see note 202), pp.39–43, 78–9; see also Rafael (see note 182), p.41

207 Jackson (see note 202), pp.43–5; Rafael (see note 182), pp.42–4; Burns (see note 201), pp.90–1. For the report of UN observers on the Khan Yunis raid, see UN Security Council Official Records, 10th year, Supplement for July to September 1955, pp.8–11

208 Quaker House Committee, 26 September 1955, minute BQH 51

209 On this and subsequent paragraphs, see Sydney D. Bailey, 'A Case-Study in Quaker Mediation', *Friends Quarterly*, vol. 26, no.2 (1990), pp.88–95

210 Mordechai Gazit, *The Peace Process*, 1969–73, Jerusalem, Hebrew University, 1983, pp.12, 107–8, 122

211 Published studies of recent Quaker mediation-reconciliation are as follows: Roland L. Warren, 'The conflict intersystem and the change agent', *Journal of Conflict Resolution*, 1964, pp.231–41; Landrum R. Bolling, 'Quaker Work in the Middle East following the June 1967 War' and C. H. 'Mike' Yarrow, 'Quaker Efforts Towards Reconciliation in the India-Pakistan War of 1965', in Berman and Johnson (see note 189), pp.80–110; Yarrow (see note 54); Sydney D. Bailey, 'Our vocation of reconciliation', *Friends Quarterly*, 1980, pp.244–9; Jackson (see note 202); Roland L. Warren, 'American Friends Service Committee Mediation Efforts in Germany and Korea' and Landrum Bolling, 'Strengths and Weaknesses of Track Two Diplomacy: a personal account' in McDonald and Bendahmane (see note 189), pp.27–34 and 53–64; T. J. Pickvance, 'Third-Party Mediation in National Minority Disputes: some lessons from the South Tyrol Problem', in *New Approaches to International Mediation*, ed. by C. R. Mitchell and K. Webb, London, Greenwood, 1988, pp.131–46; Bailey, 'A Case-Study in Quaker Mediation' (see note 209); Bailey, 'A Quaker initiative to end the Korean War' (see note 187); Thomas Princen, *Intermediaries in International Conflict*, Princeton University Press, 1992, pp.186–252. Among the case-studies in *Quaker Experience of Political Mediation*, QPS, 1990, are those on Zimbabwe by Trevor Jepson, East-West Relations by Roland Warren, and Northern Ireland by Steve and Sue Williams. There is also a strictly confidential manuscript by Walter Martin about mediation efforts regarding Southern Rhodesia-Zimbabwe in 1978–80. More general studies from the past half century include Pickard (see note 136); Pickett (see note 74), pp.401–20; Ullmann, *The Dilemmas of a Reconciler* (see note 160); Robert O. Byrd, *Quaker ways in foreign policy*, University of Toronto Press, 1960, pp.181–92; Adam Curle, *Making Peace*, London, Tavistock, 1971; Wolf Mendl, *Prophets and Reconcilers*, Swarthmore Lecture 1974, Friends Home Service Committee, 1974; Wood (see note 82); Adam Curle, *True Justice*, Swarthmore Lecture 1981, Quaker Home Service, 1981; Martin (see note 190); Sydney D. Bailey, 'Non-official mediation: reflections on Quaker experience', *International Affairs*, 1985, pp.205–222; Adam Curle, *In the Middle*, Leamington Spa, Berg, 1986

212 Yarrow (see note 54), pp.62–5, 262–4; *Quaker experience of political mediation* (see note 211), case 3, p.4; Bailey, 'A Case-Study in Quaker Mediation' (see note 209), pp.90–2; Berman and Johnson (see note 189), p.81; Pickvance (see note 211), pp.131–2, 142; Yarrow (see note 54), pp.262–4

213 Jackson (see note 202), pp.11, 17–8, 22–5, 40–1, 81, 97; Warren (see note 211), p.236; McDonald and Bendahmane (see note 189), p.28; Berman and Johnson (see note 189), pp.83, 100; Yarrow (see note 54), pp.123, 127, 166, 190, 195, 249; *Quaker experience of political mediation*, (see note 211), Case 1, pp.2, 5; Case 5, p.6

214 Yarrow (see note 54), pp.100, 127–8, 166, 250, 256, 267–9, 272, 278–9; Bailey, 'Non-official mediation' (see note 211), pp.210, 211, 212, 214, 215; Martin (see note 190), p.974; Curle, *In the Middle* (see note 211), p.14

215 Bailey, 'Non-official mediation' (see note 211), p.216; Jackson (see note 215), pp.50, 53; Yarrow (see note 54), p.129

216 'A "Border Incident"', *The Friend*, 14 August 1970, pp.951–2

217 Curle, *In the Middle*, (see note 211), pp.9, 27; Warren (see note 211), p.232; McDonald and Bendahmane (see note 189), p.28; Miller (see note 158), p.46

218 Hugh Thomas, *The Suez Affair*, Harmondsworth, Pelican ed., 1970, p.151

219 *The Complete Diaries of Theodor Herzl*, ed. by Raphael Patai, New York, Herzl Press, 1960, vol. 2, pp.573, 579

220 Curle (see note 211), p.18; Martin (see note 190), p.974; Berman and Johnson (see note 189), p.99; Jackson (see note 202), p.79

221 *Ibid.*, pp.40–2, 78–9; Berman and Johnson (see note 189), p.109; Yarrow (see note 54), pp.22–24; 198, 201, 209–13, 233, 253–4; *Quaker experience of political mediation* (see note 211), p.6

222 Horace Alexander, 'Peacemaking . . . a Lifelong Occupation', *The Friend*, 23 July 1948, p.609; Yarrow (see note 54), p.266

223 2 Corinthians 5: 18

224 Yarrow (see note 54), pp.138–9, 258–9

225 *Ibid.*, pp.102, 136; Curle, *In the Middle* (see note 211), p.11; Berman and Johnson (see note 189), p.6; McDonald and Bendahmane (see note 189), p.54

226 *Quaker experience of political mediation*, (see note 211), Case 1, p.4

227 Tinker (see note 192); Yarrow (see note 54), pp.250, 289; Ranjit M. Chetsingh, 'A letter from India', *The Friend*, 8 October 1965, pp.1215–6

228 Yarrow (see note 54), pp.25–6, 161; Berman and Johnson (see note 189), p.96

229 Yarrow (see note 54), pp.86–90, 226–30, 275–6; Martin (see note 190), p.975; *Quaker experience of political mediation*, (see note 211), p.4 and Case 1, p.3; Southern Africa Working Group, 17 November 1976, minutes

230 Oran R. Young, 'Intermediaries: additional thoughts on third parties', *Journal of Conflict Resolution*, 1972, pp.59–61

231 Curle, *In the Middle* (see note 211), p.11

232 *Quaker experience of political mediation* (see note 211), p.9

233 *Ibid.*, p.10

234 *The Friend*, 10 September 1965, pp.1074–5; 8 October 1945, pp.1215–6

235 Yarrow (see note 54), p.205; *Quaker experience of political mediation* (see note 211), p.18; Case 1, p.5

236 Yarrow (see note 54), p.24; Jackson (see note 202), pp.26, 34, 97; McDonald and Bendahmane (see note 189), pp.29, 56; Pickvance (see note 211), pp.136–7; Curle, pp.10, 25; Alexander (see note 222), p.610

237 Berman and Johnson (see note 189), pp.84, 87; Yarrow (see note 54), pp.112–3, 123, 216; Curle (see note 211), p.20

238 Jackson (see note 202), pp.39, 42, 43, 44, 45, 46, 49, 53, 56; *Foreign Relations of the*

United States, 1955–57, vol. XV, pp.328, 754

239 UN General Assembly Official Records, 46th session, Supplement no.1, p.2

240 Yarrow (see note 54), p.165; *Quaker experience of political mediation* (see note 211), Case 1, p.9; Jackson (see note 202), pp.47–8, 53–55, 97–8

241 Warren (see note 211), p.237; Berman and Johnson (see note 189), p.30

242 Warren (see note 211), p.239; McDonald and Bendahmane (see note 189), p.30

243 Jackson (see note 202), pp.32, 39, 40, 49, 53; Yarrow (see note 54), pp.257–8; Martin (see note 190), p.974; Curle (see note 211), p.16; *Quaker experience of political mediation* (see note 211), p.9

244 *Ibid.*, Case 1, p.8

245 Patrick Seale, *Abu Nidal: gun for hire*, London, Hutchinson, 1992, pp.162–3, 263–4, 304

246 Scott (see note 61), pp.204–5; Hughes (see note 71), pp.85–91; Bailey 'Our Vocation of reconciliation' (see note 211), p.248; *Quaker experience of political mediation* (see note 211), p.17; Martin (see note 190), pp.974–5; Warren (see note 211), p.240

247 Yarrow (see note 54), pp.135–6, 273–4

248 Jackson (see note 169), pp.137–45; Jackson (see note 202), p.85; *Quaker experience of political mediation* (see note 211), p.6

249 Garret FitzGerald, *All in a Life*, London, Macmillan, 1991, p.473. The Michael referred to was Michael Lillis

250 Jackson (see note 202), pp.77–8; Yarrow (see note 54), p.255; Curle, *True Justice* (see note 211), p.55

251 *On the manner of negotiating with Princes*

252 Jackson (see note 202), pp.27, 29, 36, 81; Bailey, 'A case-study in Quaker mediation' (see note 209), p.92

253 Berman and Johnson (see note 189), pp.82, 104; Yarrow (see note 54), pp.76, 77, 108, 160, 170, 252; Curle, *True Justice* (see note 211), p.60; Bailey, 'Non-official mediation' (see note 211), p.211; Curle, *Making Peace* (see note 211), pp.16, 28; McDonald and Bendahmane (see note 189), p.58

254 William Conrad Gibbons, *The US Government and the Vietnam War*, Washington, D.C., US Government Printing Office, 1988, part II, pp.56–7. The Westerner was McGeorge Bundy (President Johnson's National Security Assistant), the Asian was Tri Quang (President of the Association of Buddhist Monks). The conversation took place in Saigon in February 1965

255 *Journal of Palestine Studies*, 1974, p.215; Jimmy Carter, *Keeping Faith*, London, Collins, 1982, p.379

256 Jackson (see note 202), p.36; Berman and Johnson (see note 189), p.106; Yarrow (see note 54), pp.174, 254

257 McDonald and Bendahmane (see note 189), p.29; *Quaker experience of political mediation* (see note 211), p.8

258 UN Security Council Official Records, 11th year, Supplement for April to June 1956, p.44

259 Warren (see note 211), pp.239, 240; McDonald and Bendahmane (see note 189), pp.31, 81; Berman and Johnson (see note 189), pp.92, 108–9; Yarrow (see note 54), pp.156, 170–1, 201; Martin (see note 190), p.274; Curle, *In the Middle* (see note 211), p.7

260 Jackson (see note 202), pp.51, 113–5; *Quaker experience of political mediation* (see note 211), p.15 and Case 1, p.8

261 Yarrow (see note 54), pp.76, 193, 232, 235; Curle, *In the middle* (see note 211), p.11; Odd Bull, *War and peace in the Middle East*, London, Cooper, 1976, p.113
262 Martin (see note 190), p.274
263 William E. Barton, *The moral challenge of Communism: some ethical aspects of Marxist-Leninist Society* (Swarthmore Lecture 1966), Friends Home Service Committee, 1966; Barton, 'Ethical Aspects of the Christian-Marxist Dialogue', in *What kind of revolution?*, ed. by James Klugman and Paul Oestreicher, London, Panther, 1968, pp.73–98
264 Published in *Christianity and Crisis*, 13 June 1955, reprint distributed by the Church Peace Union, New York City; Pickard (see note 136), p.26
265 Bailey, 'A case-study in Quaker mediation' (see note 209), p.92
266 Warren (see note 211), p.236; Curle, *In the middle* (see note 211), p.12; Yarrow (see note 54), p.173
267 Jackson (see note 202), pp.50, 77; *Quaker experience of political mediation* (see note 211), Case 1, pp.1, 9, 10; Yarrow (see note 54), pp.99, 112–3, 137, 204, 206, 210, 217
268 Curle, *In the middle* (see note 211), p.6; Jackson (see note 202), pp.39, 82; Yarrow (see note 54), pp.209–10; *Quaker experience of political mediation* (see note 211), Case 2, p.2
269 Jackson (see note 202), p.9; Bailey, 'A Quaker initiative to end the Korean War' (see note 187); Yarrow (see note 54), pp.250–1
270 Jackson (see note 202), pp.36, 38, 45, 47, 49, 51, 52, 54, 78, 82, 83, 84, 85, 98; Yarrow (see note 54), pp.113–5, 194, 196–7, 198, 199, 200, 214, 234, 255
271 Carter (see note 255), p.366
272 UN Security Council Official Records, 4th year, Special Supplement no.7, pp.130–41
273 Warren (see note 211), p.238; Yarrow (see note 78), p.165; *Christian Faith and Practice . . .* , 1960, §571
274 Genesis 12: 11–20; 26: 7–11; 27: 11–29; 1 Samuel 28: 7–14; Acts 5: 1–11
275 *Reminiscences of Levi Coffin*, Cincinnati, 1876, pp.35–41, 301–4, 335–6, 457–8, 464–70, 548–51, 552–3, 606–8
276 Eberhard Bethge, *Dietrich Bonhoeffer*, London, Collins, Fount ed. 1986, pp.717–8; Dietrich Bonhoeffer, *Ethics*, London, Collins, Fontana ed. 1964, p.364
277 Letters from Ellen Friis, 11 January, 8 and 13 March 1992
278 For a perceptive review of the ethics of deception, see Sissela Bok, *Lying*, New York, Pantheon, 1978
279 *Quaker experience of political mediation* (see note 211), p.18
280 1 Corinthians 12: 4–11; 2 Corinthians 5: 19; Ephesians 4: 4–7, 11–12
281 Warren (see note 211), pp.232–3; Berman and Johnson (see note 189), p.90; McDonald and Bendahmane (see note 189), pp.29, 56–7
282 Berman and Johnson (see note 189), pp.98, 108, 109; Yarrow (see note 54), pp.164, 175
283 UN Security Council Official Records, 38th year, Supplement for July to September 1983, pp.102–3, S/16005*; Riaz M. Khan, *Untying the Afghan Knot*, Durham, N.C., Duke University Press, 1991, pp.48, 117–8, 290
284 William B. Quandt, *Decade of Decisions*, Berkeley, University of California Press, 1977, p.241
285 Jackson (see note 202), p.85; Bailey, 'a Case-study in Quaker Mediation' (see note 209); Yarrow (see note 54), p.277; Curle, *In the middle* (see note 211), pp.49–50

286 Wilson (see note 55), pp.24–5; Wilson (see note 40), pp.12–3
287 Yarrow (see note 54), pp.261–4
288 Isaiah 6: 8
289 Edward H. Milligan, 'Quaker Service', *Friends Quarterly*, vol. II (April 1948), p.94
290 Alexander (see note 192), p.609
291 Matthew 19: 21; 6: 34; 6: 19
292 For a fuller expression of this idea, see A. E. Harvey, *Strenuous Commands*, London, SCM, 1990, pp.161–8, 208–10